"A TREE OF LIFE"

THE HISTORY OF **The Memorial Foundation**

Text by

Jay Sheridan

Photography by
Pulitzer Prize-winning photographer

Robin Hood

Contributing photographers

Peyton Hogue

Rich Kalonick

Hunter Armistead

Bill Steber

GRANDIN HOOD
Publishers

ACKNOWLEDGEMENTS

The publisher expresses a sincere appreciation to Beth Seigenthaler Courtney, President, and Sonya Watson, Senior Art Director, of DVL Seigenthaler for their generous support and counsel, and for providing archival photography of the Memorial Foundation.

A special thanks to Linda and John Tanner of Madison, both former employees of Nashville Memorial Hospital and stewards of the Nashville Memorial Hospital Archives, for providing archive photos from the Hospital's history.

THE HISTORY OF
THE MEMORIAL FOUNDATION

Designed by Robertson Design, Inc.
Franklin, Tennessee
www.robertsondesign.com

Published by:
Grandin Hood Publishers
1101 West Main Street
Franklin, Tennessee 37064
www.grandinhood.com

Printed in China through Four Colour Print Group, Louisville, Kentucky

ISBN: 978-0-9908184-8-9

TABLE OF CONTENTS

Like the families it served, Nashville Memorial Hospital was continually growing and expanding its reach, adding beds, medical equipment, ambulatory capacity and other facilities to better accommodate the booming population. The Physicians Office Building was one of the first major expansions in 1976.

DEDICATION: J.D. ELLIOTT

BY WILLIAM B. PURYEAR, IMMEDIATE PAST BOARD CHAIR EMERITUS

After living with a person for nearly half a century, you get to know that person very well.

We were fortunate enough at Nashville Memorial Hospital to find an extraordinary person to lead us at a time of greatest need. Against all odds, we opened a hospital across the river from much of the population of Greater Nashville, in an area with few referring physicians. Our initial patient population was thirty, in a hospital for one hundred and fifty. Not only were we under water financially, but our organization and personnel were stressed as well.

J.D. Elliott came to us with a solid background in hospital administration, and the effect on our personnel's morale was immediate and obvious.

J.D. made those around him feel better about themselves, with his ready smile and infectious wit. He came bringing peace and optimism to all who worked with him.

It was my privilege to work with him as an officer and then chairman of the board as he brought cheer and harmony to the environment. His familiar voice on my early first call every morning was a tonic to begin my day. Over these years I came to know him as well as I did anyone on this earth, with the exception of my wife—who happens to be a lot like him—and I can truly say he was one of my closest friends. Through his wisdom in making recommendations to the board of approval of grants, which were almost always accepted, he brought hope and faith in the future to those whose hopes were often wan. Not just to our hospital and foundation did he bring such hope; his managerial talents and community spirit were quickly recognized by all, which led to many positions of honor and service, and he spread his talents generously over all of these.

As a tribute to J.D.'s lifetime of charitable spirit, I am honored to dedicate this book to his memory.

He and my wife were two of the kindest, gentlest, and most optimistic persons. It has been my privilege to know and work with him for fifty years.

My best friend, J.D., is terribly missed.

—William B. Puryear
Immediate Past Board Chair Emeritus

The Memorial Foundation

MISSION STATEMENT

To improve the quality of life for people through support to nonprofit organizations.

FOREWORD

Dear Friends,

Looking back on twenty-two years evokes a range of emotions. Certainly, while we felt sure we were doing the right thing in selling Nashville Memorial Hospital to create the Memorial Foundation, we could not have anticipated the depth and breadth of impact that has taken place since 1994.

Reading through these pages, we are reminded of the people who make this region great. Among them are some of those visionaries—men and women who were involved in the campaign to raise the funds to build Nashville Memorial Hospital, who steeled their resolve through the sale and transition, and have served the Foundation faithfully. There are many more whose spirits have transcended their time with us on earth, and many more still who continue to give their time and talents to support the Memorial Foundation.

And then there are the beneficiaries, more than 825 agencies who have received over $148 million in awarded grants since the Memorial Foundation was started. Reading their stories, it is heartening to read that the support has often come in the form of something other than funding—a hand in shaping the vision, of evaluating effectiveness, of encouragement and affirmation.

Looking back, we remember those organizations who might not have survived, or gotten off the ground, or those who were so close to making great things happen, and through the Foundation's support have made a lasting impact for people in need. And we are pleased to read of how the bar has been raised in the non-profit community as a result of the accountability that our board has required of its beneficiaries. Our community is better for it.

None of it would be possible without the dedicated staff that worked at Nashville Memorial Hospital and the staff here at the Memorial Foundation. And we learned from the best: J.D. Elliott. J.D. was a humble man who always led by example, letting his actions speak for themselves. You'll see the fruits of his labor seeded throughout this book, and we will forever appreciate the years we spent together.

After his death in 2015, the board established the J.D. Elliott Leadership Development Fund, an initiative we believe will allow his actions to continue to speak for generations to come, and build upon his legacy by giving people filled with passion the skills and wisdom necessary to turn vision into reality.

Reflecting on twenty-two years, perhaps this best encapsulates the Memorial Foundation: turning vision into reality, cultivating seeds that become mighty oaks, believing in people and organizations who are dedicated to serving the greater good. Collectively, the impact is staggering.

Please enjoy flipping through these pages, as we chronicle the struggles and the victories of a great community, led by remarkable people. We speak for the board and staff of the Memorial Foundation in saying it has been our greatest pleasure to be a part of it.

Scott S. Perry
President

William P. Puryear
Immediate Past Chair Emeritus

Frank Grace, Jr.
Board Chair

History

THE NOT-FOR-PROFIT NASHVILLE MEMORIAL HOSPITAL WAS ESTABLISHED TO SERVE THE DESPERATE NEED FOR QUALITY CARE ON THE EAST SIDE OF THE CUMBERLAND RIVER. IN THE YEARS TO COME, THE NATIONAL HEALTHCARE LANDSCAPE CHANGED DRAMATICALLY, AND IN 1994, THE HOSPITAL WAS SOLD. A NEW HOSPITAL TOOK ITS PLACE, AND THE MEMORIAL FOUNDATION WAS ESTABLISHED. AS A RESULT, MORE THAN $148 MILLION HAS BEEN SEEDED INTO THE NASHVILLE COMMUNITY OVER THE LAST 22 YEARS TO HELP THOSE WHO NEED IT MOST. HERE IS OUR STORY.

A DREAM FULFILLED

More than 100,000 people lived on the east side of the Cumberland River in 1959, across communities interspersed with farmland stretching from Inglewood to Madison, Goodlettsville, and out to Donelson. That number represented a full quarter of the Nashville area's population, yet very little was available in the way of health care.

A charter was filed that year, when an idea for a non-profit community hospital began to develop among a young general surgeon with deep roots, Jeff Pennington, M.D.; a British architect named Don Cowan new to town, having married a Nashvillian; and Bill Willis, a respected attorney with an interest in the city's promising role as a center for health education and management. Bill Puryear, a certified public accountant by trade, would serve the fledgling group as treasurer. Amon Evans, the publisher of the *Tennessean*, would be asked to chair the Board of Governors.

What tied the alliance together, beyond a common mission of delivering quality care to people who desperately needed it, was that each was willing to work for free to make it happen. An exploratory committee came together to begin assessing the viability of raising the money and galvanizing the political will that would be required. Private conversations were held, temperatures were taken, and loyalties were formed. And while those involved recount the very real struggle of the early months and years, they recognize it was a home run waiting to happen. Quietly, the concept for Nashville Memorial Hospital began to come together, including a prime piece of real estate in Madison.

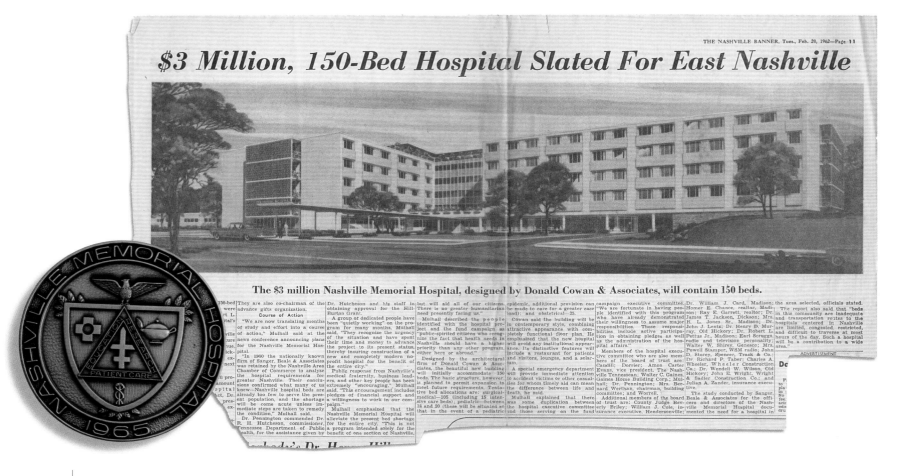

THE NASHVILLE BANNER, Tues., Feb. 20, 1962—Page 11

$3 Million, 150-Bed Hospital Slated For East Nashville

The $3 million Nashville Memorial Hospital, designed by Donald Cowan & Associates, will contain 150 beds.

The urgency of the need was undeniable. Not only was there no hospital, but few doctors practiced on that side of the river. A consulting firm hired to do a feasibility study in 1960 reported a shortage of more than 100 beds over and above the 241 beds initially envisioned for Memorial Hospital, and that Nashville would need 225 additional beds within another five years. Dr. W.T. Sanger, the national hospital consultant, echoed city and county officials who said the city needed not only more beds but specialty facilities to serve outside referring communities if Nashville was to maintain its reputation as a regional medical center. Statistically, one out of every eight citizens would be hospitalized within a calendar year.

Sanger's report cited a 25- to 27-minute trip in an ambulance during rush hour, with the siren screaming, to transport an emergency patient from the east side of the river to the west, and to the nearest hospital. "We need that hospital," a veteran ambulance driver told the *Tennessean*, "and we've needed it for years."

Meanwhile, the City-County Planning Commission's data projections showed the area's greatest population growth on the east side, particularly in the vicinity of White's Creek, Antioch and Joelton. It was the byproduct of plentiful land, accessibility to the new interstate highways, the proposed Percy Priest Lake, and the availability of public water and sewer for new subdivisions. Officials estimated then that the area around Old Hickory, Goodlettsville, and sections of Pennington Bend that were largely farmland could grow by 4,000 percent over the next fifteen years.

The morning daily quoted one administrator at a large Nashville hospital explaining that, as a rule, most patients had to wait eight or nine days to be admitted to the hospital, and as long as three weeks for a non-emergency. This was the situation all over the city, she said, not just at her hospital.

A new hospital, according to Board members and a growing contingent of opinion leaders, would address that medical service vacuum in a way that could mean the difference between life and death. One physician recalled a case where a patient who presented with a growth was not considered an emergency; by the time he was admitted more than a week later, the growth had doubled in size. It proved to be cancerous.

Nashville Memorial Hospital President J.D. Elliott and Chairman of the Board J.E. Malone

On the larger scale, there was a vision among civic leaders to increase medical manpower in an area of the metropolitan region that was dangerously short on physicians, to create flexible employment opportunities for non-working nurses and support staff, to provide more beds for the infirm and others requiring specialized care— including those from outside the area or state. Clearly, it would positively impact the model across the entire city.

"Nothing unites a community like a common purpose, a common objective," Sanger said. "A common goal such as this could do much to erase any 'barrier' of a river."

By February of 1962, when the fundraising campaign officially commenced, not only had the Chamber of Commerce endorsed the concept, but so had the governor, the state commissioner of public health, the county judge, and the city-county health

Nashville Memorial Hospital under construction ca. 1964

director—all agreed there was a need, and the logical place to meet it was on the 28-acre tract of land already secured in Madison.

At the press conference announcing the initiative, Dr. Pennington revealed a tentative allocation of 52 percent of the project's cost through federal Hill-Burton health care development funds. It was up to the local community to raise the other $1.5 million needed.

The launch of the capital campaign was a sight to behold. Dozens of members of the founders' organization executed a well-organized blitz of business, government, civic, faith and medical interests with detailed memorial and naming gift opportunities, pledge cards, and letters of intent. Soon, there were teams working in neighborhoods and social circles all over the city, with a goal to complete the effort by Memorial Day. Missing that target only seemed to embolden the captains, lieutenants and foot soldiers, who were armed with prospect lists, talking points and campaign manuals, even pledge suggestions to deliver to employers based on the size of the company. By July 1, they had crossed the $1 million mark.

If there had been any doubt that the city at large could be sold on the value of a hospital on the other side of the river, it had all but evaporated. Women's organizations were having bake sales and bridge tournaments, church groups were passing the offering plate, neighbors were going door to door, and a rodeo was held, complete with the live auction of a prized bull. Every penny went to support the hospital campaign.

Ad campaigns soliciting support turned into employment ads, and the excitement around the new Memorial Hospital—the first of its kind, a self-sustaining non-profit, not requiring the support of any government, institution or corporation—was palpable. As the July 1 Grand Opening approached, the subject dominated the news. On June 28, 1965, the afternoon *Nashville Banner* recounted a dedication ceremony the day before with more than 1,000 in attendance.

Man's Humanity to Man...

Nashville Memorial
HOSPITAL
A non-profit community organization

"Believe It Or Not"

Here are some important facts about life expectancy.

At the time of
Julius Caesar—life expectancy
1850
1900
TODAY—life expectancy is

26 years
38 years
48 years
71 years

The advancement of medical science and the improvement of HOSPITAL CARE have brought us longer, healthier and happier lives.

To meet the needs of our rapidly growing population the Board of Trust approved the construction of a 211 bed hospital. This decision increased the bed capacity of the hospital by 41% and gives the community a hospital which can be operated with greater efficiency and greater economy to stem the rapid rise of hospital costs.

Nashville Memorial
HOSPITAL

1962
150 beds

1964
211 BEDS

Madison's new hospital offered the very latest in systems and technology, promising the highest level of care and comfort for its patients when it opened on July 1, 1965.

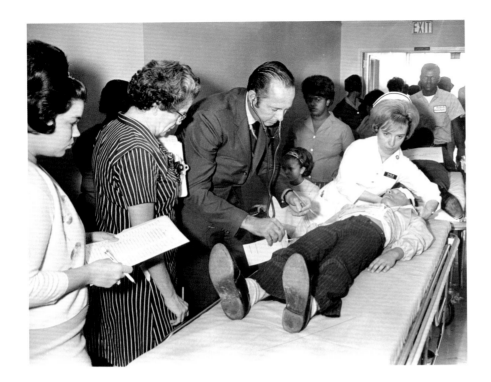

As a non-profit hospital, Nashville Memorial was dedicated to education and community engagement, like this disaster drill held on Oct. 8, 1969.

John D. Tanner, RT (ARRT) conducts a skull exam on July 14, 1965.

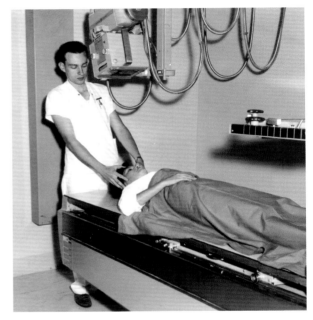

When the hospital campaign was first announced in 1962, the plan called for 162 beds. However, the rapidly growing population quickly demonstrated that a larger facility would be needed to adequately accommodate the expanding service area. By the time the hospital opened in 1965, the capacity had increased by 41 percent, to 211 beds.

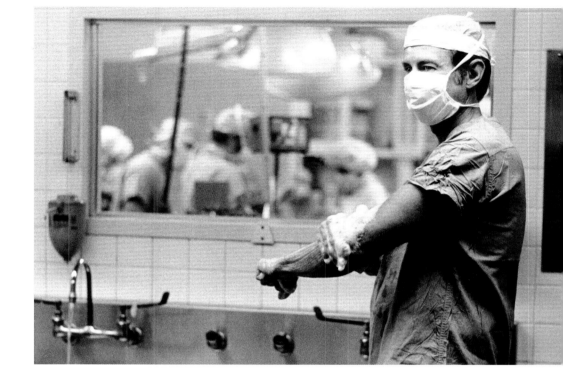

Joining the members of the Board on the dais were the state's two United States senators, Nashville's congressman, the governor and the mayor, along with President Johnson's undersecretary for Health Education & Welfare, Wilbur J. Cohen, who delivered the dedicatory address.

Congressman Richard Fulton acknowledged the skeptics who said it couldn't be done, while Governor Frank Clement said it symbolized what can be accomplished when "people of every political persuasion and from all walks of life combine their efforts in one great purpose."

Perhaps Senator Albert Gore was the most prescient that day.

"This hospital reinforces my pride in helping write the Hill-Burton Act [under which the hospital ultimately received nearly $2 million]," Gore said. "Now after a long, hard fight, we are about to cross the last milestone of a program to make possible the paying of medical costs by untold millions of people in the evening of their lives."

Barely a month later, Medicare was passed into law. Before the year was through, more federal legislation would signal a torrent of dramatic changes that would transform the face of health care and the way it would be financed in America. Among them: the implementation of the Civil Rights Act of 1964, Social Security-funded medical benefits for the aged and disabled, and grants to the states for medical assistance programs. In 1966, it was wage and hour laws that established provisions for overtime.

The year 1970 brought OSHA to the table, with its stiff regulations and penalties, and the same year saw price freezes and other industry controls in response to the impending recession. Subsequent years would bring sweeping change to everything from organized labor to medical malpractice laws, and the prospect of a national health insurance model.

Despite the challenges, Nashville Memorial Hospital thrived. Hospital President J.D. Elliott announced 15 percent growth in admissions in the 1969 Annual Report; even as he cautioned against continued cost pressures, the prognosis was good. A decade later, Elliott reported that the hospital was building physical facilities at a faster pace and providing more quality care for more people from more geographical areas than ever was dreamed of in 1965 when the hospital opened.

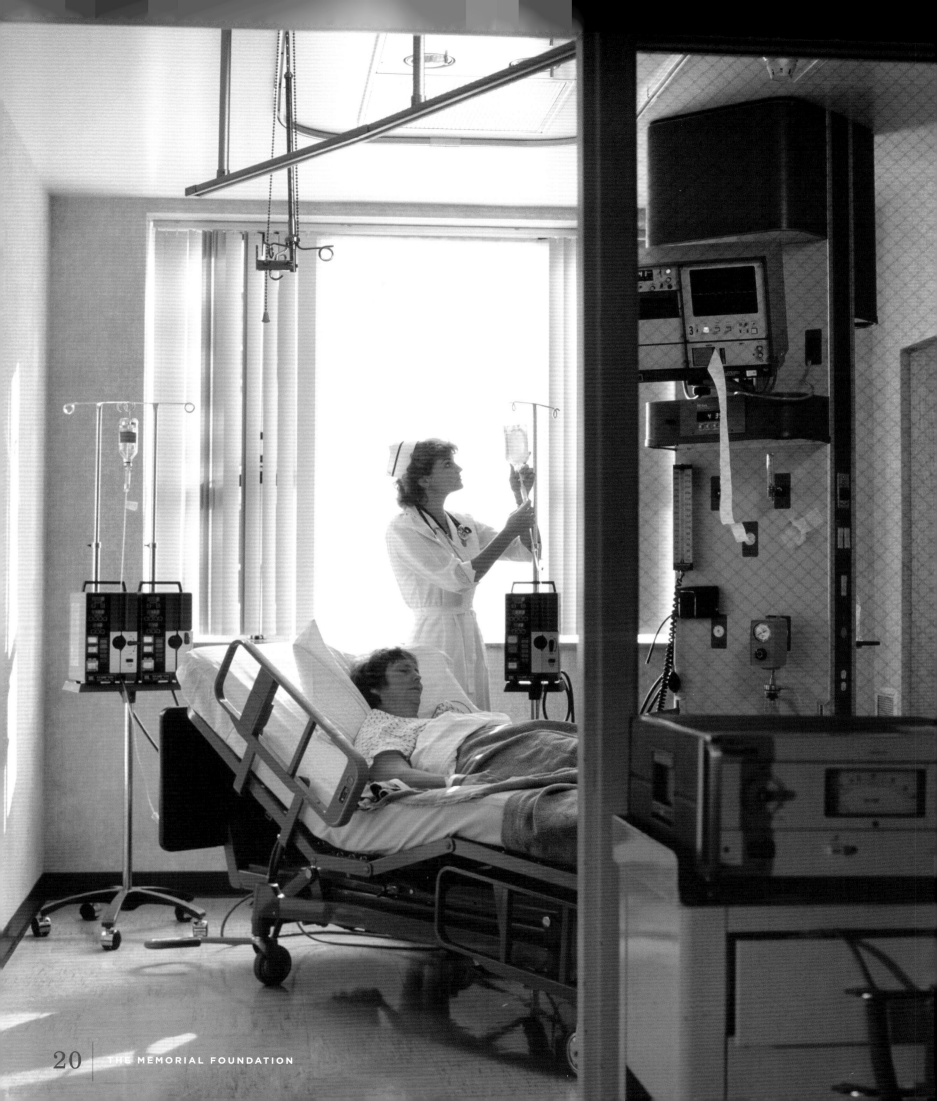

Five years into operation, future needs had begun to emerge, and studies led to blueprints. In 1976, a new patient wing and physicians office building were opened. More than 650 people were now employed at Nashville Memorial, supported by nearly 300 volunteers. Yet the Tennessee Hospital Association's 1965–75 report showed an average annual increase in the cost of providing a day of care up 18.5 percent, and advances in medicine and technology were driving life expectancy up and mortality down. The phenomenon of recession combined with inflation, coupled with public debate and government intervention, promised to continue challenging the bottom line.

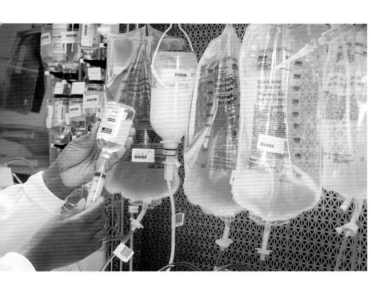

Still, the unbridled growth continued, with new CT scan equipment, additional operating rooms and a 16,000-square-foot outpatient services building soon brought online. Nashville Memorial now boasted the largest emergency department in the city, seeing more than 100 patients every 24 hours.

The fiscal year 1982–83 was dubbed the "year of change," with the Annual Report detailing a complete corporate restructuring that would maintain the hospital's non-profit status but install for-profit outpatient, ambulatory, pharmacy and other service companies underneath the umbrella of Nashville Memorial Health Systems, Inc. The average occupancy had grown to nearly 90 percent—80 percent was a great number a decade before—and Medicare/Medicaid now represented more than 40 percent of the average patient days. It was a move designed to "take charge of the future," according to Chairman of the Board Bill Puryear.

"We will decide on new and expanded directions so that it may be said, 'Nashville Memorial Hospital moved at the right time, planned for the future, and helped create a better, more comprehensive healthcare system for the people,'" Puryear said. That year, a new heart lab opened, approval was gained for cutting-edge cancer radiation therapy, and the latest CT scanner was installed.

Nashville Memorial Hospital President J.D. Elliott addresses the camera at a press conference, ca. 1976. At left, the Physicians Office addition gleams.

Opposite: Nashville Memorial Hospital's "Cain-Sloan Caper" Day was held September 26, 1974, at the popular department store's Rivergate Mall branch to benefit the hospital. Cutting the ribbon that day were (Left to Right): Mrs. Beverly Briley, Congressman and Mrs. Richard Fulton, J.D. Elliott and Mrs. Todd Francis.

Twenty years in, the hospital was seen universally as a success. Game-changing shifts in reimbursement models, rapidly advancing technologies, the growth of outpatient services, changing demographics, and even the use of desktop computers created a new frontier, and with it came even more significant legislation. Through it all, the hospital continued to grow and succeed, while keeping patient costs low. With no investors or shareholders to answer to, the motivations were pure.

"We will give our patient-customers high tech and a human touch, with convenient access to all avenues that lead to good health," Puryear said in the 1985 report. "This community hospital will continue to give its 'shareholders'—the people—an attractive return for their support and trust."

In that anniversary year, ground was broken on another physicians' office complex to house expanded outpatient diagnostic and treatment services, while the laboratory staff performed more than 20,000 procedures each month.

The next decade would bring even more change, notably to the way hospitals were being managed, and Nashville was at the center of it. By 1993, an American hospital industry long driven by government, religious and academic institutions was seeing an explosion of investor-owned hospitals, and with it mergers and acquisitions as facilities tried to figure out how to compete with one another. Nashville Memorial was the exception, free from debt and with a large cash reserve, a respected medical staff and state-of-the-art services, but it was becoming clear that it would be difficult to keep up with the industry over time.

Two Decades and Growing

Our Tradition of Community Service Continues

At Nashville Memorial Hospital, we are a community of neighbors and friends who provide medical care for those we know, or get to know, and love. The name of this new publication reflects that spirit of community and concern.

Each issue will tell us about each other, the traditions that are special to us, and "new" traditions, such as NEIGHBORS & FRIENDS, that we are just beginning to establish.

In 1985, our 20th anniversary year, we have continued our tradition of striving for excellence as we care for our patients. More than 6,000 have come through our doors and found attention to their medical, emotional, and spiritual needs.

Our rehabilitation programs, short-stay surgery, and outpatient diagnostic services have allowed members of our communities to receive hospital treatment without being hospitalized. Our Emergency Room staff has provided "right-now" treatment when there was no time to wait.

The medical staff continues a tradition of excellence. This year, fifty-four physicians, representing specialties ranging from family practice to critical care, have joined more than 200 other doctors who practice at our hospital.

The volunteer spirit at Nashville Memorial increases with each passing year. During 1984-85, our volunteers donated some 32-thousand hours of their time and talents.

We continue our tradition of health education for our communities. Children visit us to learn about hospitals and lessen their fears, to learn about first aid, to overcome their speech and learning difficulties. They come for seminars and workshops that help them learn how to learn.

Support groups ranging from Alcoholics Anonymous to the Lupus Foundation meet each month at Nashville Memorial. Other regularly scheduled programs include diabetes education, CPR courses, classes for expectant parents, weight loss, exercise and fitness, and cardiac and pulmonary risk factors and rehabilitation. Senior citizens, more than 100 of them, come to the hospital each month for a day of information and fellowship.

We continue our tradition of growing and changing to meet the needs of our communities. Last summer, we broke ground for the multi-million dollar Health Resources Center, which will house new outpatient diagnostic areas, an oncol-

treatment center for radiation therapy and chemotherapy, a new location for an expanded Due West Pharmacy, and additional medical offices.

Employers throughout the mid-state area will find reduced health care costs for their employees through our participation in preferred provider organizations such as Signature Health Alliance, HealthMaster, HealthNet, and Care-Choice.

We could not continue established traditions or begin new ones without the efforts of our Board of Trust. These dedicated civic leaders, who volunteer their expertise and guidance, offer us wise counsel and lead us in directions that benefit all of our communities.

At Nashville Memorial, we...

best wishes for a blessed holiday season and a healthy and happy new year.

Sincerely,
J.D. ELLIOTT
President

Radiologist Dr. William Hill, NMH President J.D. Elliott, Board of Trust Chairman William P. Puryear, general contractor George Buchanan, Jr., and architect John Preston (from left) break ground for the hospital's new Health Resources Center.

Neighbors & Friends

NEIGHBORS & FRIENDS at Nashville Memorial Hospital is published four times each year by the Department of Marketing and Public Relations and is directed to the hospital's employees, physicians, volunteers, and special friends. J.D. Elliott, President, Nashville Memorial Hospital. Matt Newbill, Vice President, Marketing. EDITOR, Mary Newbill, Director, Public Relations. DESIGN...

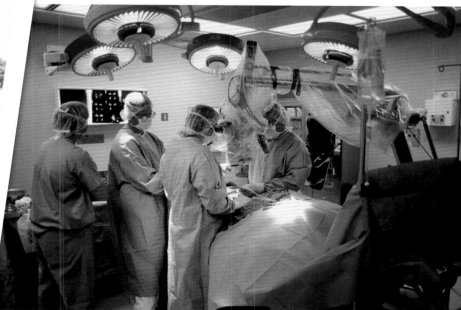

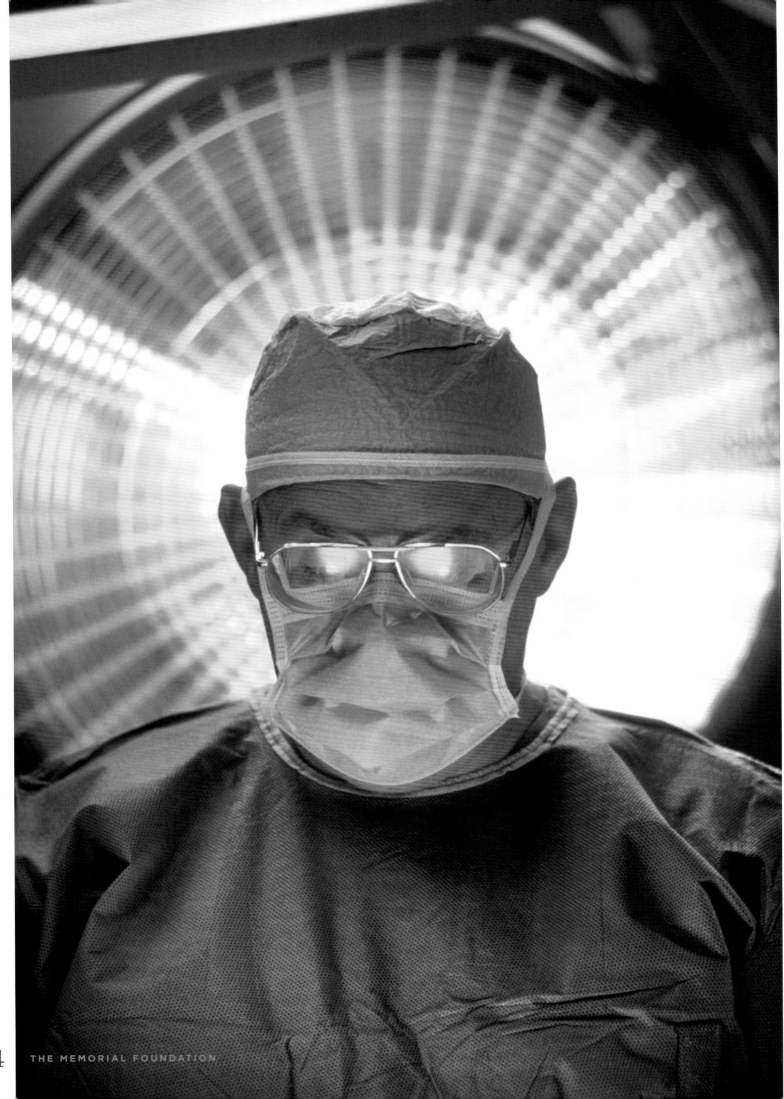

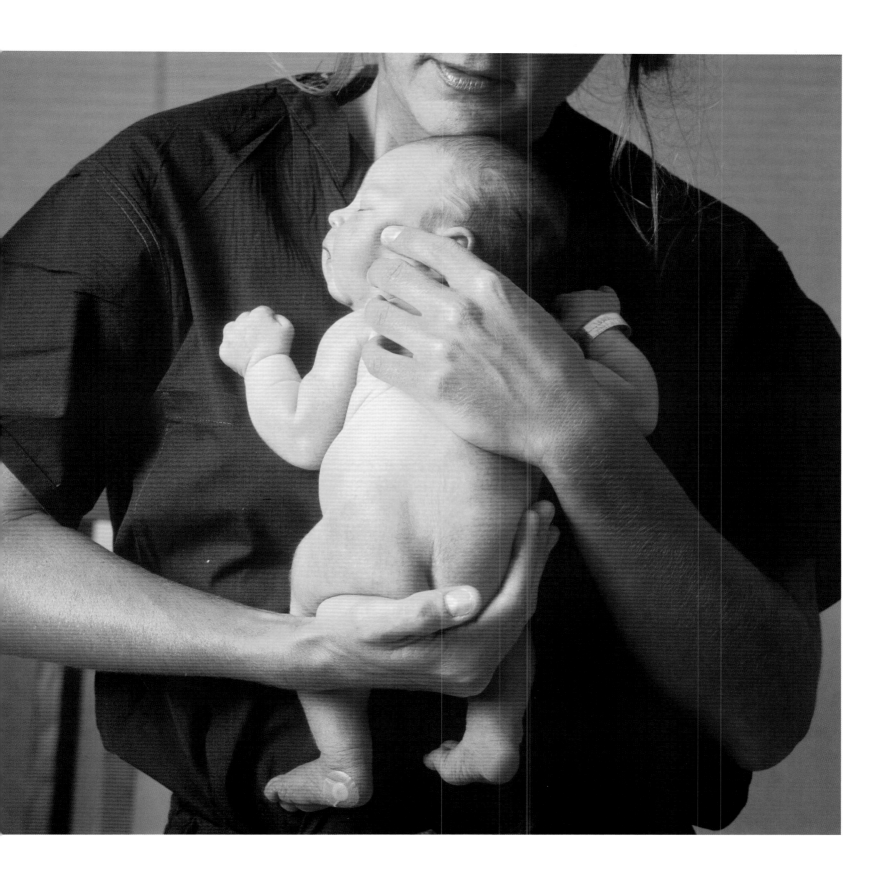

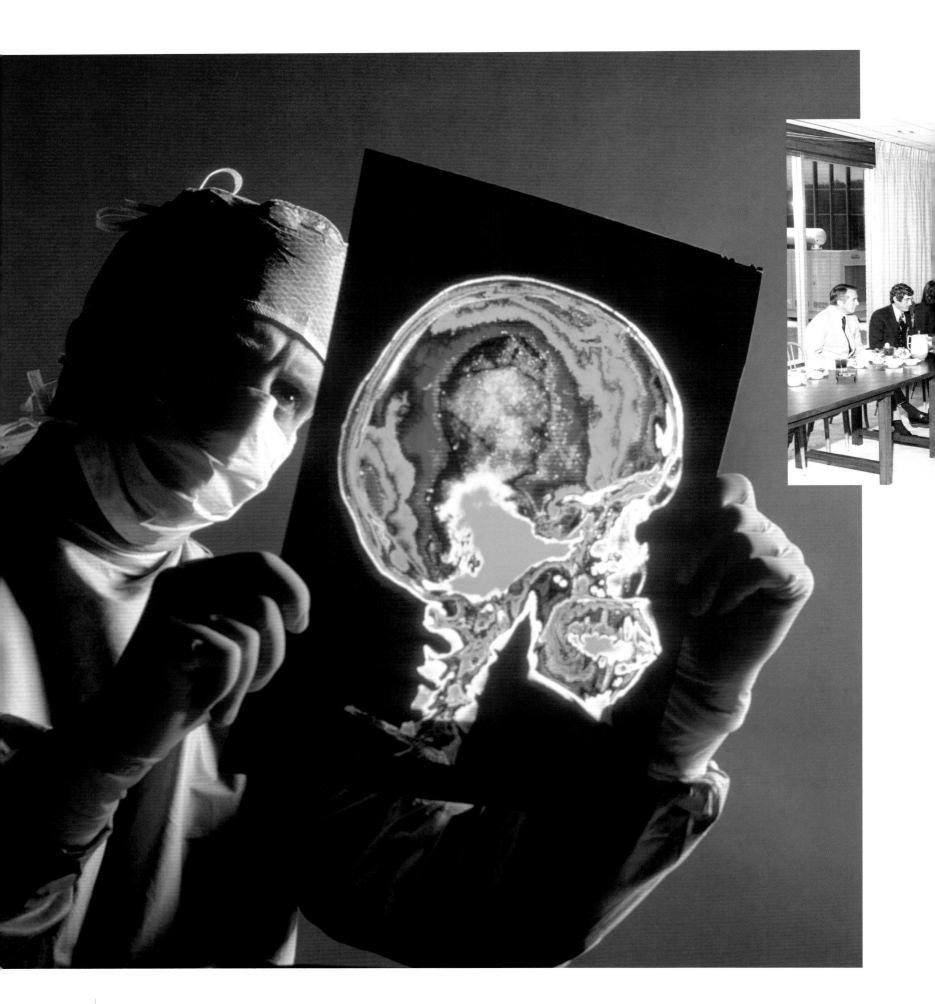

The Board of Trust met regularly, and often on the agenda was the purchase of new medical equipment to serve the constantly growing need and rapid advances in technology. Such was the case at this meeting in the 1970s.

"We could see that it was going to be very challenging to generate excess reserves for capital expenditures, and with no corporate base for donations and support," President J.D. Elliott said. "I took a chance and met with the chair and vice chair of the Board, and we began discussing the fate of a non-profit hospital serving working class people, while Medicare patients were increasing and reimbursements were decreasing.

"There were 14 Board members and I went to each one of them and talked about how it could benefit the community if we sold—the community would get a better hospital and the support of a new foundation that could make a significant impact for years to come."

Elliott's administrative team was working with HealthTrust at the time to bring to market a preferred healthcare model; the company was headquartered here but did not own a Nashville hospital, and expressed an interest in purchasing Memorial. As the confidential conversations continued, Elliott would come in to the office on nights and weekends to make copies of due diligence without raising an alarm, and he ordered a fairness evaluation from the investment banking firm J.C. Bradford.

In April of 1994, as the $42 million hospital sale was approved unanimously by the Board, the Memorial Foundation was established. In addition to the proceeds from the sale, the Foundation would retain the cash reserves, property, assets and receivables, all told totaling $105 million.

A competing not-for-profit hospital along with five individuals, including two doctors and three citizens, filed suit attempting to block the sale, claiming the board had acted improperly. After an exhaustive investigation of the hospital's history and operations, and with the authority of the state statutes to make that determination, in the best interest of the public. the state attorney general ruled in favor of the sellers. As a non-profit, there were no members, and the Board had the sole authority to sell.

J.D. Elliott, the hospital's president since its inception, was out of work.

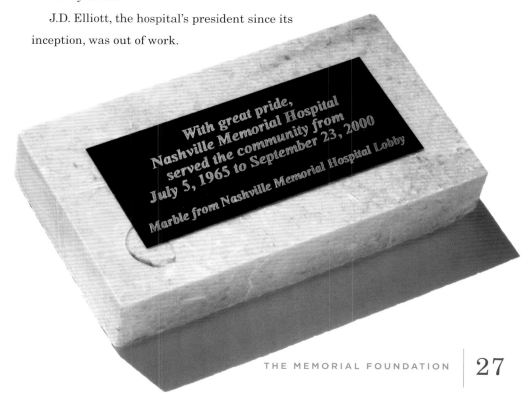

With great pride,
Nashville Memorial Hospital
served the community from
July 5, 1965 to September 23, 2000

Marble from Nashville Memorial Hospital Lobby

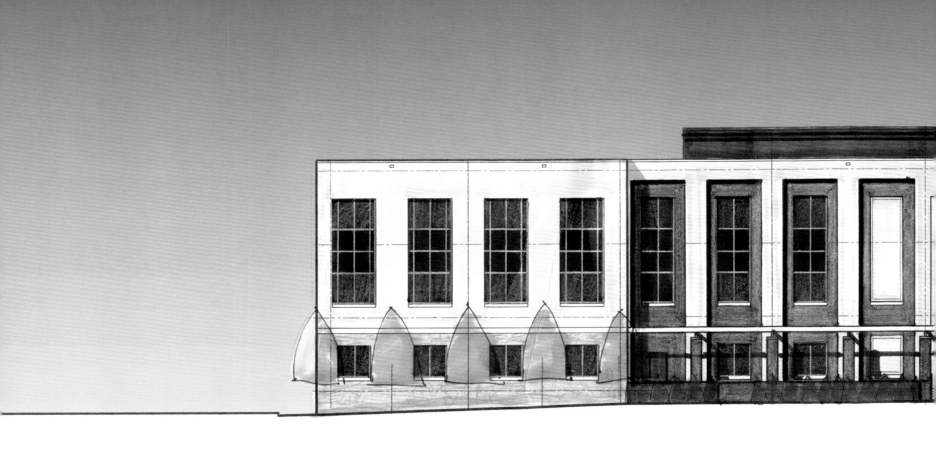

"It was a difficult thing to do, and I could have walked away or ridden it out for a number of years. But I felt like it was necessary to at least consider for the benefit of the hospital and the community it served," he said. "If you're the CEO of a company, do you want to move it forward, stay status quo or decline? I felt like I was doing my duty."

After a nationwide search for an executive director of the Memorial Foundation, Elliott's loyalty—along with his passion and his expertise—was rewarded. The newly formed Board of Directors (which comprised the former hospital Board members, plus seven new additions) arrived right back where they had started, with the right man for the job.

The first meeting of the Memorial Foundation Board centered on priorities, and some broad initial focus areas emerged: education, senior citizens, social services, and disadvantaged and troubled youth. Many of the directors had been involved since the fundraising campaign of 1962, and they never lost sight of the people who had played a role. The women's auxiliaries, the Sunday School classes, the line workers…each of them had felt a sense of ownership in the hospital. How could the Foundation benefit the community that had given so much?

As the legal elements were finalized, Elliott and his Board worked to establish a vision, policies and procedures to study other foundations, best practices and investment protocols that would safeguard the principal while driving a return on the investment. The fully funded hospital employees pension plan was converted to annuities and established a two-percent annual increase for each member.

By 1996, the grant-making process was ready to begin, and the inaugural project was identified. The Memorial Foundation would build a new senior center for the citizens of Madison, right in the heart of the community. Financing was allocated for both the construction and the operations moving forward. The 50 Forward program was born, and twenty years later, residents who rely on the Senior Center still remember its genesis. After all, these were the people who had raised the money, provided the care, birthed children and been made whole at Nashville Memorial Hospital.

It would be the first of hundreds of programs, initiatives, causes and facilities that would be launched, improved—even saved—by the Memorial Foundation every year, with gifts large and small. Each year, the guiding principles are reviewed, but they've stayed constant. Amid all the change and development that Nashville has experienced, the need has only increased.

The newly formed Memorial Foundation would start making grants in 1996 and in 2003, build its headquarters at Bluegrass Commons in Hendersonville. (L-R) Foundation President J.D. Elliott, Stan Hardaway of Hardaway Construction, Kem Hinton and Steve Johnson of Tuck-Hinton Architects, Crews Johnston of Colliers Turley (realtor).

It ranged from children to those under care of hospice, to schools and libraries, medical clinics for the less fortunate, resources for those recovering from addiction or incarceration, new residents assimilating into a new culture and language, generational Nashvillians in need of clothing or utility assistance or temporary housing, even environmental causes.

Some are one-time gifts and others are longstanding relationships. But none are multi-year commitments—each organization must apply every year, and demonstrate that they accomplished what they said they would.

Among the highlights of service on the board of the Memorial Foundation are semi-annual site visits, where beneficiaries showcase the fruits of the support received, and the people whose lives are touched share their stories. Here, board members visit the Oasis Center in 2015. In the basement of the facility the Memorial Foundation helped fund is a bicycle repair shop, where teens engage their minds and hands as part of the therapy program.

Any worthy mission serving Davidson, Sumner or Robertson County making a request receives a full evaluation from the Board, who gauges the need and the promise against the Foundation's priorities before making a grant decision.

Over two decades, through the tech bubble of the '90s and the recession and strife of the 21st century, the Memorial Foundation has carefully cultivated the proceeds generated by a single community hospital into one of the largest foundations in the region.

Across the peaks and valleys of the American economy, the Foundation has tightly adhered to its determination to distribute five percent of the endowment's average value through grants each year—these days, that means several million dollars are seeded year after year into the community, putting other organizations in a position to be successful in their critical work.

J.D. Elliott had contributed a half-century of service to the Hospital and the Foundation when he passed unexpectedly on July 22, 2015, having suffered from complications after a routine surgery. The week before, he had been meeting with grantees and evaluating their effectiveness and accountability, while giving his personal time to numerous civic organizations, non-profit organizations, as an elder at his church, and as a husband, father, grandfather, and great-grandfather. The year before, and the one before that, he had been recognized by his peers as one of Nashville's Most Admired CEOs, the kind of affirmation most often reserved for those who eschew it.

His legacy of service is the personification of the Memorial Foundation, and amazingly, he was not alone. Elliott and his Board were deliberate about recruiting diverse perspectives who bring value to the work, but many of the directors go back to those days in the 1960s, when the question was asked: How best can we serve this community?

Mr. Elliott said it best, looking back on twenty years in the 2014 Annual Report. Having contributed over $135 million to worthy non-profits across Middle Tennessee, it was only the beginning of the growing season.

"We resolve to stay the course, regardless of what the future holds. Next year—and in all the years following—we are determined to remain a place where giving grows."

Thus is the significance of the Memorial Foundation, as unique and wonderful as the city it serves. The following pages contain only a few highlights of the people and the organizations who have improved millions of lives cultivating those seeds, each of them simply united in humanity.

The staff of the Memorial Foundation (Left to Right): Vice President for Programs and Grants Jackson Routh, President Scott S. Perry, Executive Assistant Joyce A. Douglas, Vice President for Finance Judy Milliken, and Receptionist/Secretary Donna Kay Vick.

THE BOARDROOM

WITH THREE HUNDRED AND SEVENTY-FIVE COMBINED YEARS OF SERVICE, THE EIGHTEEN DEDICATED MEMORIAL FOUNDATION BOARD MEMBERS HAVE AWARDED MORE THAN 3,800 GRANTS TO MIDDLE TENNESSEE NON-PROFIT AGENCIES AND SERVICES.

Board Member Profiles

RARELY DOES AN INDIVIDUAL SUSTAIN A PASSION FOR SERVICE AS A
BOARD MEMBER FOR MORE THAN A FEW YEARS. BUT THE MEMORIAL
FOUNDATION IS NO TYPICAL NON-PROFIT. AMONG ITS DIRECTORS ARE
MEMBERS WHO HAVE SERVED SINCE THE CAMPAIGN TO RAISE FUNDS
TO ESTABLISH NASHVILLE MEMORIAL HOSPITAL IN THE 1960S. AND
MANY MORE COUNT THEIR TERM OF SERVICE BY THE DECADES. AMONG
THEM ARE TEACHERS, ACCOUNTANTS, EXECUTIVES AND PHYSICIANS,
YOUNG AND OLD, UNITED IN A COMMON PURPOSE: PROVIDING
CRITICAL FUNDING TO OUR CITY'S MOST IMPACTFUL CHARITIES. MEET
THE DRIVING FORCE BEHIND THE FOUNDATION.

BILL PURYEAR

SERVICE SINCE *1962*

Bill Puryear says the world is full of too many fascinating things. Now in the twilight of his storybook life, having been a writer, painter, geologist, musician, philosopher, and Certified Public Accountant, he's as active as ever.

"I wanted to be all those things, and so I've kept at them throughout my life," Puryear says. "Those diverse interests have been the source of much joy over the years, and I am fortunate to be in a position to continue doing what I love every day."

Puryear is the son of a judge and a school teacher, a Korean War veteran, and a native of Gallatin whose roots stretch back to the 1780s and General William Hall, who replaced Sam Houston as governor of Tennessee when Houston left for Texas. That connection to the place he loves is reflected in his writing and artwork, including acclaimed books on local history and oil paintings that reflect his research and travels. His farm overlooking the Cumberland River is a trove of artifacts and mementos.

While the noted accounting firm that carries his name may have been his professional legacy, the story goes deeper. Puryear founded the Tennessee Marble Company, for instance, which supplied material from an East Tennessee mountain vein for landmarks far and wide, including the National Gallery of Art in Washington, D.C.

Yet one might argue that his work with the Memorial Foundation has been as significant as anything. Puryear served as chairman of the board at Nashville Memorial Hospital, and later as chair of the Foundation's board, and can now claim more than a half century of service to the cause.

"The Foundation was birthed in strife," he says with conviction. "We were the first to sell a non-profit hospital and create a charitable foundation with the proceeds, and that was not without controversy. But we believed in what we were doing. Our goal was not publicity, but was instead to give some sponsorship to those who don't have any—poor children and their parents, people getting out of prison with no job or hope, those afflicted by disease or circumstance … basic needs that help people and give them dignity."

He mentions the Salvus Center in Gallatin, which provides free medical care to the disadvantaged, Vanderbilt Children's Hospital, the Reading Room at the downtown Nashville Public Library that serves as many homeless looking for respite and inspiration as it does children learning the wonders of prose. He's been a big advocate for Pope John Paul II in Hendersonville, the private Catholic school that is putting kids who couldn't afford that kind of education into the Ivy League. These are among the hundreds of organizations and untold numbers served under his leadership, and that of the board and staff he led.

Today, he might be working on another book or capturing the scenes of Middle Tennessee present and past on canvas, while treasuring the memory of his wife of sixty years, Claudia, twelve grandchildren, and one great-grandchild on the family farm. He looks forward to Memorial Foundation board meetings each month and still manages a few investments for clients, and you never know what other project might have attracted his talents and passions, but regardless, the result will be exceptional. Lord willing, he'll be doing the same for many more years to come.

DREW MADDUX

SERVICE SINCE *1962*

Overlooking the fields where champion thoroughbreds were once raised, Drew Maddux tells the story of winning a pony, a saddle, and a bag of oats as a five-year-old child. His family lived in town, so the horse pastured in the yard and stabled in the garage each night. That experience stuck with him, to the point that an affinity for horse racing ultimately led to a thriving operation where his horses were bred to legends like Triple Crown–winner Secretariat.

"Sumner County land has this pocket of what's called Murray soil. In Middle Tennessee it is four times larger than the thoroughbred breeding grounds in Lexington," Maddux says. "It's high in phosphate and grows great bones in race horses—that's one reason Sumner County was the center of horse racing from the 1800s until the Civil War. It started as a hobby for us, but developed into a substantial business with up to 48 thoroughbred race horses and breeding stock."

Now retired, Maddux recounts his life and career, and those kinds of moments that sparked a passion.

"I went to four colleges and universities and didn't graduate from any of them, being a senior-year dropout, but I've been on Belmont University's board of trustees for 33 years," he says. "Back then I was holding down five jobs, riding the bus, and trying to get a degree, but I started selling real estate while in college."

By the time he was 22, Maddux owned a growing real estate company and had started building houses. At age 29, he was elected president of the Nashville Board of Realtors and voted Realtor of the Year. Over the years he built subdivisions, apartments, and major retail centers, working with his son, Drew Jr., who ultimately became the president of the Homebuilders Association of Middle Tennessee.

But despite his professional success, Maddux's legacy is rooted in what he contributed outside of business hours. That started with the idea of Nashville Memorial Hospital, back in 1959.

"Dr. Jeff Pennington and the first board chairman, Clay Gaines, came to my fledgling real estate office with this idea, and they wanted me to donate money, help raise money, and serve on the board,"

he remembers. "They didn't even have the land yet, but we all jumped in and I served as co-chair of the Building Committee. When the hospital opened, my mother and my wife were Pink Ladies and my daughter was a candy striper, volunteering there. I stayed on the board, shifted to the founding board of the Memorial Foundation when the hospital was sold, and have been a part of it ever since."

Now more than a half-century later, Maddux still serves on the Foundation board and chairs the Projects Committee. His family is as engaged as ever in serving the people who need it most. Through the Fellowship of Christian Athletes, of which he was the national vice chairman, the Madduxes have been a part of producing nearly 600 camps attended by over 100,000 children across America. For thirteen years, they packed up their five grandchildren each summer and worked at camps in Colorado, Indiana, and North Carolina.

Closer to home, he led the effort to totally fund and build—literally—the Temporary Residence for Adolescents in Crisis, a foster home for twenty-four foster girls in the Nashville area. Having worked with the kids and seen their plight first-hand, he and his wife, Judy, established the Maddux Family Scholarship Fund for foster children at Belmont University. Out of that has come meaningful, lifelong relationships with the recipients, which measure in the dozens.

"These are kids who don't have a chance. Through the Memorial Foundation, the Fellowship of Christian Athletes, and our scholarship fund, I'm constantly reminded that not everybody's as lucky as we are," he says. "I've been involved for fifty-seven years now with the hospital and the foundation, and it has added greatly to my family's life. We learned that we are more blessed to give than to receive."

ALICE HOOKER

SERVICE SINCE *1972*

Talk to any longtime Nashvillian, and they'll know the name Hooker. Aside from the professional contributions, their influence stretches from the political legacy of John Jay Hooker to the equestrian championship of Henry Hooker, and to the matriarchal and philanthropic leadership of Alice Hooker—a family that has made the city a more vibrant, meaningful, and memorable place.

It was Alice's mother, Hortense Bigalow Ingram, who was first approached about the concept of a hospital on the other side of the river. Long admired for her giving heart, Mrs. Ingram made a donation, and as the hospital approached its opening, was asked to serve on the board of directors. She suggested instead her daughter, Alice, who accepted the position, and remembers driving home from Madison after evening board meetings to take care of her own small children.

"I was on the board for a number of years but finally begged off. The hospital was doing fine, but they came to realize that the way things were going, the reserves would ultimately be used up," Hooker remembers. "Along in that period, Bill Puryear asked me to come back on the board, and shortly thereafter the opportunity came up to try to sell the hospital, which set off quite a fight."

Hooker, having been through tough elections and all that comes with them, had developed a thick skin. In the public eye, she says, one begins to care little about what the newspaper writes.

"I didn't like the insinuations being made and I was angry, not scared—we were doing something good for the community and being accused of trying to feather our own pockets. We knew the truth, and I wasn't afraid to say it, so the committee took me with them to meet with the attorney general."

In that meeting, the sole woman at the table spoke up, and she made her case. Soon after, the Memorial Foundation was born, and Alice Hooker has continued her service to the board ever since. Having been a member of countless non-profit boards through the years, Hooker understands the unique dynamic at play with the Memorial Foundation.

"There are so many eyes on these requests, and twenty people a month really debating and evaluating them. That's a rare thing, and we've done it without allowing politics to penetrate our culture," she says. "I'm proud of a whole slew of projects, from the work we've done to support Vanderbilt Medical Center as a teaching hospital to helping seniors and children and women. The community's health and welfare has always been at the top of the list."

She's seen the positive results on behalf of prisoners, troubled teens, and battered spouses, the historic places and rural communities and cultural and environmental treasures that have been preserved and introduced to scores of people who otherwise may have never had the opportunity.

"I think we've been so effective because one of our major objectives is to help ensure that everyone has a quality of life, even when the minimal standard is all that is acceptable," Hooker says. "It's been a very rewarding experience to have worked with these board members all these years for the cause. Now my daughter Lisa is in that generation of those in their 50s who are starting to be in the position we were back then, when we were really able to start to make an impact. It's exciting to see the cycle occur across the generations."

CHARLIE FENTRESS

SERVICE SINCE *1981*

Charlie Fentress started with the Cain-Sloan company as a high school student, working at the popular Nashville department store all the way through his time at Vanderbilt University. He became a teacher and coach at Isaac Litton High School before returning to Cain-Sloan, where he worked for thirty-five years and retired as vice president of human resources and a member of the executive committee.

When Cain-Sloan was acquired by Dillard's, Fentress retired from the company and became a consultant for organizations ranging from the National Federation of Independent Business, where he served as state director, the Home Builders Association of Middle Tennessee, and the Argis Foundation, a professional organization for business people who advocate on important community issues. He had earned a law degree as an adult, and he continued to apply his experience and education in making Nashville a better place to live. Over time, he served on the boards of the Nashville Chamber of Commerce, Junior Achievement, and the Exchange Club, among others.

All of that made him the right candidate to serve on the Metro Council for a quarter-century, where his constituents elected him six times to represent the 34th district, which includes Belle Meade, Green Hills, and Forest Hills.

"The president of Cain-Sloan encouraged me to run for office back then, and I couldn't have done it without their support," he says. "I was fortunate to be in the middle of the civic side of Nashville for a long time, and now I get to play golf and run a coffee club at Whole Foods every week, where we talk politics and everything else in the world. I've been married for fifty-eight years, have two great children, and I think I've had a pretty good life."

A big part of that was his service on the hospital board and, at least since 2004, his role on the board of the Memorial Foundation. Helping worthy charities get started, keep growing, and execute important initiatives has been deeply rewarding, Fentress says.

From the perspective of someone with a pulse on the region and a long view of Nashville's growth and development, he sees a non-profit community that is uncommonly strong and diverse.

"I think there are a lot of organizations that would not have made it without the Memorial Foundation's support," he says. "J.D. Elliott was so good at evaluating where to invest our resources, and thanks to his leadership, we have always measured results in a way that ensured they were in a position to be successful."

As a senior member of the Foundation's board, he talks of his admiration and gratitude for the early leaders, as well as the younger members who have gotten involved in recent years.

"It's such a mix of keen thinkers and different worldviews, with everyone bringing something to the table. That obviously includes the staff," he says. "It's people who have made the Foundation as significant of a player as it has been over the last twenty years. I'm a personnel guy, and I understand as well as anyone that efforts like this simply aren't possible for any length of time without the right people involved. It was a brilliant strategy and vision, and I'm thankful to have been a part of it."

FRANK BUMSTEAD

SERVICE SINCE *1985*

Inside Frank Bumstead's office, photos and mementos of the A-list personalities he's worked with over the years tell of a successful career in the Music City. Only Bumstead is not an artist, a producer, or a record label executive. His firm fills a unique niche in the business, financial, and personal planning side of entertainment management.

"My professional path started in the '70s after I returned from Vietnam and went to grad school at Vanderbilt. I went to work for a bank and was later hired by an individual whose needs created my career," Bumstead says. "He had gained a lot of wealth, but had spent and lost a lot of it, then made more. My job was to protect him from his friends, his family, and himself in personal and business affairs. Chuck Flood, Mary Ann McCready, and I started this company a few years later."

Today, Flood, Bumstead, McCready & McCarthy is known for the daily oversight and administration of the financial aspects of entertainment careers: accounting for the tickets and merchandise sold on tour, accounting for and auditing royalty receipts, contract negotiation, bill paying and investment oversight, among other aspects. With offices in New York and Nashville, their client list includes some of the most successful artists and songwriters in the industry today.

That experience was what attracted the attention of Amon Evans, then publisher of the *Tennessean* and chairman of the board of Nashville Memorial Hospital, to invite Bumstead in 1985 to join the board.

"In addition to my experience in the financial world, I had done quite a bit with clients on the healthcare services side as well," he says. "As we approached the early 1990s, we found that we had a very successful hospital—professionally and financially—but the writing was on the wall. The population of our service area was rapidly aging, Medicare was expanding rapidly, and reimbursement rates were being cut just as quickly.

"J.D. Elliott, being the unbelievably competent hospital administrator he was, said we needed to do some networking with other health services organizations on the other side of the river, and we started having those conversations."

That effort ultimately led to the sale of Memorial Hospital, and a means of continuing to benefit the community by addressing critical needs. As the new Memorial Foundation was launched, Bumstead assumed the head of the investment committee responsible for managing and growing the proceeds from the hospital's sale.

Overseeing the relationship with the Foundation's investment advisors, Bumstead encouraged broad asset allocation, understanding that the responsible approach to their financial stewardship was asset class selection, and managing for negative cycles of the economy.

"I learned an important lesson early on in my career: You make more by mitigating losses in the down time than you do outperforming in good times," he says. "In 2008, when one of our asset allocation funds was down about 10 percent, the S&P was down 37 percent, and most of the rest of the market down 40 to 50 percent. We simply lost less, and recovered more quickly."

That strategy has led to growth, more than doubling the corpus over the last twenty years, allowing the Foundation to give away over $140 million (more than the sum of the proceeds of the hospital sale) while protecting the principal and adding more than $25 million to the original fund balance.

"That's a big responsibility, and this is a truly special entity that has such a great meaning to a community in which we all live. We set out to level the playing field for economically and socially disadvantaged people, with a special focus on youth, women, and senior citizens, and supporting the health needs of those who can't afford it. I think the impact has been more broad and meaningful than any of us could have imagined, and that's an incredible thing."

DAVID McKEE, M.D.

SERVICE SINCE *1991*

David McKee wasn't raised in privilege, or even with a sense of home. As a preacher's child, McKee moved around a lot with his family, but Murray, Kentucky, is where he earned a college degree and met his wife. After working his way through medical school at the University of Kentucky and a residency in Richmond, Virginia, McKee opened an office at Memorial Hospital in Nashville.

As the only plastic surgeon practicing at Nashville Memorial, McKee was integrally engaged with the medical staff, serving over the years as head of surgery, as chief of staff, and as a member of the hospital's board of directors.

"I didn't have much experience when I arrived at Memorial. We didn't have a lot of money growing up; in fact, we didn't even have health insurance, so I'd certainly never served on a board," McKee says. "But it was a fascinating group, and so impressive to me because they had the best interests of the hospital at heart. I continue to be amazed by this group of people, who have this heart for service and have dedicated themselves to the community for decades. It's been an inspiration in my career."

McKee continues to practice plastic and reconstructive surgery at Skyline Medical Center, the hospital now serving the area, and has remained an active member of the Foundation's board since the sale of Nashville Memorial. Looking back, he says he's most amazed by their ability to understand what the healthcare landscape would look like in the future, and the difficulties that were on the horizon back then.

"We were still very much a viable hospital, but it was clear that we wouldn't be able to sustain that long-term. The times were changing so dramatically, with healthcare policy and for-profit hospitals emerging," he says. "The vision to do this while the hospital still had value was out-of-the-box thinking, and they convinced me early on. I think we were one of the first community hospitals in the nation to sell, but a bunch followed."

The results are clear, McKee says, thanks to the focus and dedication of those early leaders and the many who have supported the Foundation ever since. As the son of an evangelist who devoted his life to a singular belief, he sees that sense of purpose shining through the board and staff of the Memorial Foundation.

"There's been lifesaving work done here, and I'm proud to have played some small role. It may sound incongruous, by I've devoted my life in practice to reconstructive surgery, and that ability to transform people's lives after injury, trauma, and disfiguring disease—that's where my heart is," he says. "It just fits with the vision that my father and mother shared with me, and I've seen mirrored in the service of the Foundation.

"These people could be doing a lot of things with their lives, and they've chosen to focus on this. It's been marvelous to be a part of that process, helping people who need help. It's just a blessing to be involved."

VARINA BUNTIN

SERVICE SINCE *1994*

When a non-profit hospital was sold to create a foundation dedicated to addressing the critical needs of its community, a ceiling was shattered. Perhaps there should be no surprise in the parallel that saw a male-dominated Nashville medical world yield a philanthropic organization that was expanded to bring on people of diverse experiences—including a number of powerful women—to their leadership. Among them were Alice Hooker, who had made her own mark on the hospital board since the 1960s, and Varina Buntin, Hooker's nomination for a new foundation board member.

Wife to ad executive and farmer Jeffrey Buntin, Varina was known in charitable circles, having been the first woman elected to the board of trustees at Montgomery Bell Academy, and helped nurture and support the other schools her three children attended. Over the years, she served as a director on the board of the Ensworth School, and was named a life trustee at Harpeth Hall. She developed a passion for education, and for confronting the challenges that children of all economic and social backgrounds face: teen suicide, ADHD, autism, and others.

Buntin grew up on Tyne Boulevard, becoming a writer and meeting Jeffrey through her work. Soon they transitioned to his family farm in Robertson County, where the kids became the sixth generation to be raised. The Buntins have lived there for forty-three years now, but during the work day—and for decades—much of their time was spent in Nashville.

"I was chairing the Swan Ball (1994) and sitting in the kitchen when Alice called and said she had something she wanted me to be a part of. I really didn't need to take on anything else but I couldn't resist her, and I started right away," Buntin remembers. "I owe the fact that this foundation has become such a part of my life to her, and it is a huge honor.

"I remember saying after my first meeting how hard it was going to be to make a decision on the grant applications, and they told me it would never change. It's a big responsibility, and you commit to it knowing it's going to be a priority for you. It's a forever board position."

She cites organizations like the Jason Foundation, which started with the untimely death of a local football coach's son and has become a nationwide teen suicide prevention organization, the Magdalene House for abused women, and Monroe Harding, where kids with no parents are given a chance, even after they've aged out of their foster homes. It's about helping the people who need it most, and providing the kind of support that can drastically change a life.

"The group of men who have led this board from the beginning make it so unique and special. They loved the hospital, understood the environment, had the vision to establish the Foundation, and that love and passion is as strong as it ever was," she says. "We've gone from just healthcare for the patients right around the Madison area to impacting a much larger population of people across that region.

As a board, they've successfully "cultivated the seed corn" in a way that will continue to allow the foundation to offer significant financial support to those who serve the ones who need it most.

"The issues may change, but there are certain challenges we'll likely never eliminate, and a lot of those relate to children," Buntin says. "Our city now has a non-profit network that is making a big impact, and if we can help them help others with education or food or clothing or exposure, then we can raise up people who will serve this community well. It all starts there."

GEORGE PAINE

SERVICE SINCE *1994*

George Paine's local, national, and international experiences have given him a unique perspective on Middle Tennessee's evolving and diversifying community.

Growing up as the son of the medical director at Nashville General Hospital, he saw first-hand the challenges of healthcare delivery in a growing city. At the age of twenty-four, he served as an infantry platoon leader in Vietnam, where he was wounded and decorated. His professional life as a lawyer and judge took him to Russia, Eastern Europe, and the Far East with USAID, furthering the rule of law.

But it is perhaps his tenure as Chief Judge of the United States Bankruptcy Court for the Middle District of Tennessee that allowed him to see how critical the impact of the Memorial Foundation could be, and has been. Throughout his thirty-one years on the federal bankruptcy bench, he has seen the best and worst of it in the commercial and business world.

"We saw dysfunctional non-profits that did a tremendous disservice to the community," Paine says. "I came to believe that this was an avoidable tragedy. Fortunately, Memorial Foundation has the resources and insightful staff to remedy such problems and to enhance services to provide maximum benefit to the community served."

With his keen interest in veterans' issues, he cites Operation Stand Down as an example of an organization which, on a shoestring budget, has successfully helped thousands of honorably discharged veterans reintegrate into society.

"They're doing the Lord's work, and there but by the grace of God go I," he says.

Because of his foreign experiences, he has a similar interest in dealing with the influx of immigrants into our changing world—and he says he is truly pleased with the Memorial Foundation's support of organizations that incorporate these hardworking immigrants into the Nashville community and support them toward achieving American citizenship and its dream.

Lastly, with his and his wife Ophelia's families' long history in Nashville, he appreciates the Memorial Foundation's support of historic organizations such as the Hermitage, which maintains the legacy of Andrew Jackson, the only president to have an entire era named for him, and which educates school children about his role in our nascent democracy. Paine was immensely pleased when the Hermitage staff, realizing that the school system could not transport Nashville public school students to learn about Jackson, created innovative online programs that could be accessed in the classroom. These programs are now accessible in Nashville, in all 95 Tennessee counties, and in 27 other states.

Paine has served on the board of the Memorial Foundation since its inception, and applauds the courage of those who took the necessary steps to sell the hospital and create the Foundation despite all the controversy at the time.

"These prescient trailblazers understood the importance of the undertaking, the need it would meet in the community, and they found a way to bring it to fruition," he says. "I am inordinately proud of the Memorial Foundation as the first charitable organization in the Middle Tennessee region to require after-grant reports and site visits to ensure monies are appropriately spent. This practice is now a given with most foundations, but twenty years ago, this kind of follow-up was a novel approach."

JO SANDERS

SERVICE SINCE *1994*

For fifty-one years, Jo Sanders has been supporting healthcare in her hometown. Her interest started with a campaign to raise the funds to build Nashville Memorial Hospital, when Dr. Jeff Pennington asked her to lead a group of women in finding ways to generate financial support from the far reaches of the community.

"We worked on it for three years before construction started, having every kind of sale we could think of, speaking to different groups, trying to get it done because we needed it so badly," Sanders says. "There were about 300 of us when we started the auxiliary, all women about the same age with small children. We needed a hospital in our area that we could get to quickly, and were were going to get it built if it was the last thing we did."

Sanders says they sold everything they could get their hands on, holding raffles on donated treasures as diverse as a prized bull and a diamond ring. When the hospital opened, it was Sanders who led the candy stripers, serving as a representative of the Women's Auxiliary on the hospital's board of directors.

And she's been doing it ever since—volunteering weekly at Skyline Medical Center, serving on the board of the Memorial Foundation, and assisting the auxiliary effort.

"Over the years I've done it all—transporting lab samples, rocking babies in the nursery, filing records in the business office, working at the gift shop or snack bar of whatever they needed us to do," she says. "We didn't care; we just wanted to make it a community hospital that was as reasonable as possible for young mothers and fathers who had sick children."

These days, she's likely to be the first face people see at the front desk at Skyline, and the voice on the other end of the phone. She still serves on the board of the Women's Auxiliary, where she helps oversee a scholarship program for aspiring medical students. Recipients can earn support for each year of college, as long as a grade point average of 3.5 is maintained.

But the greatest honor, she says, was being asked to serve on the board of the Memorial Foundation.

"J.D. Elliott was like a brother to me, and he always supported what we were doing and made us want to do more because he cared," she says. "I was so proud when he asked me to serve on the board; we started from scratch and it's just grown to help so many people."

She's seen the results first-hand: when a friend of her granddaughter who spent a lot of time in her home fell into drugs and alcohol, it was the program at The Next Door that got her back on her feet.

"It's unreal to see what the Foundation has done for Nashville, and there's no way I can express how much I appreciate the opportunity to be a part of it," Sanders says, now in her golden years. "When the good Lord needs me, he'll know where to find me."

JULIE WILLIAMS

SERVICE SINCE *1994*

Dr. Julie Williams was in the middle of her tenure at Hunters Lane High School in Nashville when the Memorial Foundation came calling. It was 1994, the year the Foundation was established on the heels of the sale of Nashville Memorial Hospital, and the board was looking for new perspectives to join with former hospital board members to shape the future.

"One of my teachers recommended me as a representative of the Madison/Goodlettsville area. I was fairly active in the community, and the Foundation wanted to expand its board to include some different viewpoints," Williams says. "The Bible speaks to the fact that it's better to give than to receive, and this has been a true blessing for me, even though it's not my money. In my role as a principal and since I've retired, I've been able to refer people and organizations in need to the Foundation. It's been a two-way situation, for me personally and spiritually, and being able to connect the need with the solution."

Williams, who installed the acclaimed International Baccalaureate program for the first time in Nashville at Hunters Lane, was later drafted out of retirement to lead Maplewood out of state receivership. The woman who was named Tennessee's Principal of the Year in 2002 has been recognized far and wide for her caring, results-oriented approach. She now works as a regional educational consultant, bringing with her a long track record of turning around struggling schools. She also leads the Memorial Foundation's new schools committee.

She recognizes the value of the Foundation's role in education, often being called upon to support education initiatives that are new and unproven.

"The International Baccalaureate program at Hunters Lane was the first in Nashville, and only the second in Tennessee. It was a very expensive proposition. Most people on the Board of Education had never heard of it; yet the Memorial Foundation funded it," Williams says. "It allowed students to compete on a larger scale, and to get an education that is recognized throughout the world. As a result, several Hunters Lane students have matriculated to the Ivy League and other colleges that they would have never been able to attend. Thanks to the Memorial Foundation, the program has expanded to include three public high schools in Nashville."

With the inception of charter schools, the Schools Committee has researched trends and talked with business and education interests to understand the need and the potential for a solution. According to Dr. Williams, that kind of action-oriented approach is what allowed her to achieve such impressive outcomes.

"That was just one grant, but it's an example of the way the Foundation will take a chance on new initiatives, and a lot of times all these organizations need is a start," she says. "But the accountability is there. I've served on a lot of boards, and there's usually a fair amount of rubber stamping. That's not the case here. We have mutual respect for everyone's ideas, and we may have some spirited debates, but the decisions are well thought out and endorsed by the board and staff.

"Everyone on this board has a passion for the work of the non-profit community. Mine may run toward education, and others might be toward seniors or veterans or the homeless. When all of our passions and interests are together, it creates a well-rounded, diverse board. It really enriches all of us, and the benefit to the city is almost immeasurable."

BETH LITTLE

SERVICE SINCE *2001*

Beth Little has always called Hendersonville home, and her family's history there runs deep. Having raised her children there while volunteering on community projects, it was a conversation at church that led her to the Memorial Foundation.

"I had served on some church committees with Jim Rainey, and he asked if I would consider getting involved in the Foundation," Little says. "My family had strong ties to Nashville Memorial Hospital—my grandfather was a physician and my grandmother was a candy striper who volunteered there into her 80s. I remember that well."

Rainey, who had helped raise the money to build the hospital, served on the board, and continued as vice chair of the Memorial Foundation board until his passing in 2013, understood the significance of that connection. Little was flattered to become a director in 2001.

She remembers the lawsuit over the hospital's sale, and the mixed emotions her grandmother felt back then.

"I know she would be ecstatic now with the good the Foundation's done," Little says. "I remember Dr. Frist and my grandfather, who practiced in Inglewood, talking about the formation of HCA and his fear that the insurance industry would take the delivery of care out of the doctors' hands. But it's a gift to the community that has ended up being a win-win all around."

As a member of the Audit Committee, Little marvels at the wisdom that carries through the board, and the breadth of impact that comes from a deep understanding of the community's needs.

She talks of organizations like the Next Door, which helps women with addiction issues get back on their feet, and of cultural opportunities that are provided to children who otherwise wouldn't have the means.

"You never know what is inside a child that might be triggered. They may end up practicing medicine or being an astronaut, or being exposed to different music and then becoming a musician," she says. "I remember those field trips when I was a child, and hearing violins played live for the first time. Maybe it's the Adventure Science Center, and an exhibit that helps them learn how to take care of their bodies. Some of these programs can be tough to measure, but we know they have a generational ripple effect."

In Hendersonville, a wealthy suburb not often mentioned in conversations about gaps in basic needs, it was an initiative known as Grace Place that got her attention. Today, the facility serves five women and their children, a residential program designed to provide shelter and hope. Staff there work with the women to identify their strengths and weaknesses, develop a plan to save money, and find security in their lives as part of the nine-month program. The outcomes have been phenomenal.

"That program spoke to me, and the role the Memorial Foundation played in making it possible," she says. "They understood the need and the potential, held them accountable, and now it's making a difference.

"I have been blessed to be on this board and around these mentors, strong women and men and community leaders who have the best interests at heart. They've been great examples to me, and I couldn't be more grateful."

EDDIE PEARSON

SERVICE SINCE *2003*

Eddie Pearson started his career as a public accountant, working in Bill Puryear's firm and watching his mentor manage a non-profit hospital as chairman of the board. Pearson would leave after six years to help launch the Nashville-based healthcare technology company InForum, but that early experience with Puryear would come full circle years later.

"He's a special man, and I remember being so impressed with his level of dedication to the hospital as a volunteer board member," Pearson says. "It was sixteen years later that I truly understood the level of commitment these men and women have in operating the Memorial Foundation."

Growing up in Sumner County, Pearson always had a sense of pride in Nashville Memorial Hospital. Through his professional life, he later found himself serving alongside Puryear on the board of Pope John Paul II High School in Hendersonville. And as a healthcare executive, he had watched the transition from hospital to foundation with interest. That totality of experience made him a perfect candidate when the Memorial Foundation expanded its board in 2007.

Now, as chief operating officer of Healthstream, Inc., and head of the Foundation's Audit Committee, Pearson sees the significance of its role in the city's growth and development even more clearly.

"My career has been built on looking at information and data that helps healthcare organizations make smart decisions, that allow companies to take limited resources and maximize their effectiveness," he says. "Looking back, the odds were against Memorial Hospital, particularly in this market. Now having seen this community get a brand-new hospital along with a foundation that gives away several million dollars a year in support of dozens of agencies doing critical work, I don't see how anyone could consider it anything other than a win-win: we're helping people in need, only through a different venue."

From the outset, he says he noticed the service mind-set of the Foundation's board members, which mirrored the spirit he'd seen in Puryear's leadership years earlier. Likewise, the beneficiaries are providing support where it didn't otherwise exist. Take the Hand in Hand program at Pope John Paul II, where students with intellectual disabilities are paired with a student "buddy" for all four years of high school, the kind of initiative that Pearson says has brought out the best in the school's student population.

The same can be said for non-profits who serve seniors, women, and children with assistance on a level not previously possible. All of it snowballs, as one thing builds upon another.

"I call it the ripple effect, like a pebble in a pond, and it really goes back to the wisdom and dedication of this board. They understand the market, the need, the political landscape and how to bring the right people to the table to really effect positive change," he says. "You don't see that active involvement in very many places, and the Foundation has been able to tap into that passion in a really unique way. Being from here and having raised my family here, it was easy to get excited about. It was contagious, and it's become a source of pride for all of us."

NORMAN SIMS, M.D.

Norman Sims grew up in the Madison community, graduated from Litton High School and Vanderbilt University, and left middle Tennessee for the first time to attend medical school at the University of Tennessee-Memphis.

It was there that he was commissioned into the U.S. Navy Reserves, which took him to Charleston, South Carolina, upon graduation, and later to a residency in orthopedic surgery at the Navy hospital in Philadelphia and a stint at DuPont Children's Hospital in Wilmington, Delaware. After serving his six years in the Navy, Dr. Sims returned to civilian life in 1970 and began practicing orthopedics at Nashville Memorial Hospital.

He joined Dr. Jerry Hunt and a couple other doctors there, and the team later became Memorial Orthopedic Group, which had a lot of success. But an article in a 1982 medical journal would catch his attention, and alter the direction of his career dramatically.

"I was reading about the Arabian American Oil Company looking for doctors to staff its hospital there, so I took kind of a sabbatical from practice in the states and went to Saudi Arabia for a year. When his time was up, he returned to Nashville, but his interest for doing something different had been piqued. Dr. Sims re-activated with the Navy and transferred to the U.S. Air Force, and was assigned to a hospital in Germany for three years and later the Air Force Academy in Colorado Springs. His final duty station was the Little Rock Air Force Base in Arkansas, where he was hospital commander before he retired from the military with the rank of Colonel.

Dr. Sims and his wife, Margaret, would move from Little Rock to Nashville and back again twice, working with Veterans Administration hospitals in both cities. He also spent five years as vice president of medical affairs at Nashville Memorial Hospital in the early '90s.

"We were in Little Rock when Margaret became ill, and all of her doctors were in Nashville," he says. "I had served on a committee evaluating the sale of the hospital and I realized the outlook for a non-profit facility was bleak. Still I was surprised at first by the decision to sell."

The results of that decision, however, demonstrated that it was the right one to make, Sims says. Projects that benefitted education and children stand out most in his mind, such as The King's Daughters Child Development Center in Madison that provides child care and education programs for children from financially challenged families.

FRANK GRACE

SERVICE SINCE *2008*

Frank Grace remembers the earliest days of Nashville Memorial Hospital. As a partner with Bill Willis at Willis and Knight, the hospital's law firm, Grace was involved in everything from contracting to construction projects, applying for Certificates of Need for new diagnostic equipment and representing the hospital on various legal matters.

Along with independent counsel, he helped guide the hospital's leadership through the sale and the scrutiny of the state's attorney general and the establishment of the Memorial Foundation, including the national search that ultimately landed on J.D. Elliott as the Foundation's executive director.

"There were some very impressive candidates, but J.D. was the right candidate. He knew the community like no one else, and he really had his finger on the pulse of the need," Grace says. "J.D. was a quiet fellow, but he was one of the most effective people I've ever known—very perceptive, seeing issues and needs before others would—and he knew how to manage people. He cared about his work, and he had the finesse to manage personalities and expectations and processes with a great deal of tact."

Grace left Willis and Knight in 1995, but throughout his career, the impact of the Memorial Foundation was evident all around him. He joined the foundation's board in 2008 and now serves as its chairman, a role he says has been deeply gratifying.

"Even knowing the Foundation's work, I was surprised and pleased to see the breadth of contributions being made. Not just dollars but the range of agencies and services supported," he says. "That extent of the need was an eye-opener, and the way that the non-profit community has become so much more effective over the years."

Grace says the vision of the board and leaders like Elliott has yielded a far more sophisticated foundation, and by extension, the cultivation of countless organizations that have been mentored into meaningful resources. Area non-profits have been conditioned to understand accountability, and efficient operations, and their ability to raise their own funding. Many have been given small grants in a moment of great need, and then leveraged that support into thriving, integral organizations.

Looking at his board, Grace sees a group of passionate people who have dedicated much of their lives to their work with the Memorial Foundation— decades of institutional knowledge combined with focused expertise that newer members have brought to the table.

"There are members of this board who have been involved for a half-century, who helped raise the money to build the hospital, others who joined twenty years ago when the Foundation was formed, and still others who came on later and added different perspective and expertise," Grace says. "Some of those people went through hell, being sued personally and excoriated in the press and public. I believe most of the people who opposed the sale had the public good in mind, and they just had a hard time getting around the concept.

"Ultimately the community got a better hospital and the Foundation has continued to deliver care to the core service area, on a much deeper level. I think everyone recognizes the value of the Memorial Foundation today, and that's something we all can be proud of."

EDDIE PHILLIPS

SERVICE SINCE *2009*

In many ways, Nashville is still a small town, where one community leader is bound to run into another soon enough. Such was the case with Eddie Phillips and Drew Maddux, and the conduit was the Fellowship of Christian Athletes. Phillips was attending a summer camp in North Carolina with his son, and Maddux was serving on the FCA's national board of directors.

That was several years ago, and Phillips has now been a member of the Memorial Foundation board for more than five years. As a fourth-generation homebuilder and now the chairman of a development company working with his three sons, Phillips has had a lot of success, and he's been involved with a lot of non-profits across the spectrum of service offerings, from veteran care to youth engagement to homeless relief and indigent medical care.

For a number of reasons, the Memorial Foundation holds a special spot on his list of favorites.

"My mother was a candy striper at Memorial Hospital, so I remember her experience and what it meant to her when I was a child. Having served on and chaired a lot of boards, I have worked with various agencies that do great work," he says. "But if you look at the time period and figure how many organizations have been helped, the leverage is amazing. The leadership displayed at both the board and the staff levels could not be improved."

He points to people like Drew Maddux who have literally dedicated their lives to the effort, and the scenario that allowed the Foundation to give away more than $140 million and have a similar sum left remaining on balance. Compared to most non-profits that are constantly focused on raising money, the Memorial Foundation doesn't have that need to distract from its mission to help people who would benefit the most.

"Beyond the impact, the return on investment is so impressive because the staff does such a great job of holding grantees accountable," Phillips says. "The Lord has blessed the Memorial Foundation, and we've in turn been in a position to use those resources to magnify it.

"J.D. Elliott was world class, and I miss him a lot. We're very fortunate to have great leaders who can carry on that legacy. I'm just an East Nashville contractor, and I'll always be thankful for being introduced to this incredible organization."

FLEMING WILT

SERVICE SINCE *2012*

At forty-seven years old, Fleming Wilt may be one of the youngest members of the Memorial Foundation board of directors, but as a lifelong Nashvillian and the CEO over one of the city's most iconic brands and chair of his family's own foundation, he understands the significance.

Wilt is head of Christie Cookies, a family-owned business that captured the hearts of Middle Tennesseans more than thirty years ago, and today reaches a much broader market. In one of the most high-profile culinary cities in the country, the artisanal bakery market is fiercely competitive. Not only has Wilt had to find his unique advantage, but he has to manage operations for profitability.

He sees parallels with his work on the board of the Memorial Foundation, and particularly on the Investment Committee.

"Without the success of the Investment Committee, we don't have a 'business'—we don't have money to give," Wilt says. "I've known Frank Bumstead my whole life, and it's been great learning from him. Under his leadership, we have diversified the allocations and enlisted some of the best fund managers in the country, looking at the long term and constantly re-evaluating our positions. The result is a whole lot of good people doing great work for each other in this city."

In his three years on the Foundation's board, Wilt says his eyes have been opened to not only the need but the breadth of the impact. It's been a shock to see where public funding falls short for programs providing essential service to those who are suffering the most among us.

"I often think to myself, isn't this something that government should be doing a better job of addressing? Meals for school children, educational and enrichment programs, it's a critical gap that the non-profit sector is filling," he says. "We walk out of board meetings and I'm amazed at how many people we will have helped. I've always been fascinated by the metrics and the dollars per person impacted, and how we manage that process."

As one of the "young" voices on the board, he's been impressed with the ways in which the long-standing members have embraced the new Nashville. And he's learned a lot that can be applied to his other leadership roles.

"We do a lot of listening to the group who has so much experience, but they are very welcoming of our perspectives; they've made us feel like our opinions matter. We didn't live that history.

"The staff and the board working together demonstrate so much discipline and accountability, but also compassion and understanding how to be most beneficial to an organization. They must review 1,000 grant applications a year, and the institutional expertise is there to know intuitively how best to approach it. I've learned a lot that I have incorporated into my business and our family's foundation, and I'm flattered that I was offered the opportunity to be a part of it."

ALFONZO ALEXANDER

SERVICE SINCE *2013*

On the surface, Alfonzo Alexander had the world in his hands—he was the starting quarterback at Riverdale High School in Murfreesboro, which earned him a scholarship to play at Tennessee Tech, where he majored in business management. But he says he could have easily gone the other way, if not for God's grace and his mother's guidance.

Alexander started his career in human resources out of college with the Quaker Oats company before joining INROADS, which works with large companies to build internship and management training programs designed to embrace diversity among college candidates. He grew to become the regional director, with responsibility for national-level accounts, and then launched his own operations management consulting business. One of his first clients was the National Association of State Boards of Accountancy, where he now serves as chief relationship officer.

"The CEO saw that I could contribute more as a full-time executive, and I agreed. That was ten years ago, and now I oversee communications, marketing, leadership development, diversity initiatives, and more," Alexander says. "The second part of my role is serving as president of NASBA's non-profit Center for Public Trust, the ethics and leadership development arm, where we work with businesses and leaders across the nation."

His role with the NASBA also allowed him the opportunity to earn an MBA—something that marriage and fatherhood and employment had prevented after college. Alexander thought it would be another step to removing barriers for an African-American male in a leadership position.

It was through the Metro Sports Authority, the entity that oversees Nissan Stadium and Bridgestone Arena, where he was first introduced to J.D. Elliott; Elliott was being confirmed by the Metro Council for another term as a board member, and Alexander for his initial term.

"We served three years together, and every time we'd meet he'd say he just saw another grant application with my name on it," Alexander says. "I have always had a passion for non-profits and have served on several boards, and he was seeing my name on board rosters. I was intrigued by the work the Foundation was doing, and he asked if I would consider joining them."

As a busy professional, Alexander says his position on the Memorial Foundation board has allowed him to be a part of a positive impact on hundreds of organizations, rather than just two or three.

But more importantly, he sees parallels in his own life with the Foundation's beneficiaries.

"I believe firmly that God put me on the Sports Authority board to get engaged with the Memorial Foundation," he says. "My parents were seventeen years old when I was born, and my mother raised me as a single parent. Black males with this background often end up in jail or worse. My passion comes from that realization, and this is my chance to give back."

FRANK GORDON

SERVICE SINCE *2013*

Frank Gordon's career path was formed at the crossroads of healthcare and investment management. As managing partner of Crofton Capital and through senior executive roles with several healthcare companies, his work life has put him in a unique position to understand the challenges of modern healthcare.

"What J.D. Elliott put together was a model for non-for-profit hospitals to sell," Gordon explains. "The advent of the for-profit hospital industry created challenges, and non-profit hospitals became more difficult to run efficiently and profitably in certain markets. They were insightful enough to make the decision to look at the mission and explore how a charitable Foundation could serve the community in another way. Now there's a model being used all over the country, and numerous examples of hospitals who have followed this blueprint."

It's yet another sign of Nashville's leading role in the healthcare industry, and its status as an "it" city. But through his work in major markets across the country, Gordon has observed time and again that with growth comes the good and the bad.

"Needs become more acute and more difficult to address. There's always challenges, but Nashville has a long history of giving back and taking care of its own," he says. "That's something I've always been proud of about my hometown, and the Memorial Foundation has such a wide lens."

Gordon says the entrepreneurial side of the Foundation's approach attracted him to join the board two years ago, after getting to know Frank Bumstead over countless Vanderbilt basketball games. He recognized the wise leadership and counsel; the return on investment demonstrated that something special was happening here.

"Just like a capital investment in any company, we're making these grants but we're going to hold you accountable to certain milestones. We expect

judicious use of the capital, and success," he says. "JD was a terrific hospital operator, and he ran the Foundation the same way. He was a master at networking, helping people be successful, and investing more where it made sense."

Through his service on the board, he's seen the blend of institutional knowledge and fresh perspectives that have continued to keep the Memorial Foundation's finger on the pulse of the community.

"It can be tough to bring in new blood, particularly for a board that has done so well, but it was an insightful move. A lot of boards have a term of service, and that's not the case here. It's a very unique situation, and an opportunity to remain involved for the long term," Gordon says. "You have to be prepared to make that commitment, but the work is so meaningful to the city we all love."

VIRGINIA PUPO-WALKER

SERVICE SINCE *2013*

Virginia Pupo-Walker grew up the child of a Cuban immigrant, living in Nashville and understanding what it was like to be in a household where English wasn't the only language spoken.

As a student, she was fascinated by history and heritage, and she taught in Seattle and San Diego before a position as an instructor of Spanish at Vanderbilt University brought her back home. She also taught at Overton High School for four years, an experience that would shape the path of her career as a conduit between Nashville's public school system and the Latino community.

"If you speak Spanish at home but don't learn grammar and spelling, you're fluent but you don't know the mechanics. The only Spanish-language book in your home might be a Bible," Pupo-Walker says. "I focused in on Spanish for native speakers, and the byproduct is all of these conversations that emerge around being first-generation immigrants, and the issues they have with landlords, doctors, whatever. I became this sort of social-worker bridge between the community and these populations."

That role evolved into a full-time position with the Metro Nashville Board of Education, where she intersected with 85,000 children across 150 schools. She left the school system to work for Conexión Américas at Casa Azafrán, the home base for multiple agencies serving immigrant communities, where she had served on the board for five years. Her work also caught the eye of the Memorial Foundation, whose work in the educational sector was continually broadening. Soon she was asked to join the Foundation's board.

Today, Casa Azafran's headquarters on Nolensville Road is a hub of activity, reflecting not only the colorful traditions of the people it serves but also the desire of those communities to integrate into the fabric of the city.

"We work with people to start and manage businesses, on economic, civic, and social elements, on not just assimilating but integrating the best of their cultures into the American way of life," she says. "We now have culinary classes, teach English classes day and night, show them how to buy a home. We're not a food pantry—it's about teaching a man to fish."

And the children are the brokers between their parents and the larger community. They are learning English better, having to navigate taking the ACT and going to college, and embracing the chance to go beyond a trade and do something more.

"It's going to be that second generation that makes it happen, and it's already happening," she says. One of four Nashville kindergartners is Hispanic, and many of them are natural born citizens who will be eligible to vote, to become bilingual professionals, and to take advantage of a world of opportunities."

Pupo-Walker says the Memorial Foundation recognizes the importance of these elements to the future of our city, and has been a generous supporter of key initiatives that have not only helped refugees and immigrants with short-term essential services but has embraced the vision of organizations like Casa Azafran that will pave the road for thousands of beneficiaries.

"The Memorial Foundation is making an impact. Sometimes it's the seed money to start something, but perhaps more important is the credibility for organizations that comes with the support of the Foundation," she explains. "We often take the first risk, and it's inspiring to fund these tiny non-profits and change their ability to serve their objectives. Then they coach executive directors and encourage accountability, and all of a sudden that seed money has created a strong, viable organization with demonstrated outcomes in critical areas.

"It's an incredible thing to be a part of, and it's personally rewarding to be in a position to introduce the immigrant communities to a city that recognizes their value."

Beneficiary Profiles

THE ORGANIZATIONS—AND BY EXTENSION, THE CITIZENS OF NASHVILLE—
WHO HAVE BENEFITTED FROM THE PARTNERSHIP OF THE MEMORIAL
FOUNDATION CAN BE COUNTED IN THE HUNDREDS. THE NUMBER OF
INDIVIDUALS WHOSE LIVES HAVE BEEN MADE BETTER BY THAT SUPPORT
CANNOT BE CALCULATED. LIKEWISE, THE DIVERSITY OF BENEFICIARIES
DISPLAYS A BREADTH OF SERVICE THAT DEMONSTRATES THE WAY IN
WHICH A GREAT CITY TAKES CARE OF ITS OWN, FROM HEALTHCARE
TO EDUCATION, HOMELESSNESS TO ADDICTION, CONFRONTING AND
ADDRESSING THE NEEDS OF OUR MOST VULNERABLE. THE FOLLOWING
PAGES HIGHLIGHT JUST A FEW OF OUR MANY SUCCESS STORIES.

"FiftyForward enriches the lives of adults fifty and over by providing pathways to health, well-being, and lifelong learning.

—JANET JERNIGAN

EXECUTIVE DIRECTOR

FIFTYFORWARD

FiftyForward Madison Station opened its doors in 1996, addressing a critical need for social, educational, wellness, and enrichment opportunities for adults. Back then, it was the initial grant of the newly established Memorial Foundation that funded the renovation of a bank building to serve as a place where seniors from Madison, East Nashville, Inglewood, Old Hickory, and segments of Goodlettsville and Hendersonville could meet. Today, it's a bustling activity center for more than 150 daily visitors, who enjoy lively and interactive programs that allow adults in their golden years to continue leading active and healthy lives.

"I could talk all day about the great things the Memorial Foundation has done, and it's been an incredible partnership for twenty years now," says Executive Director Janet Jernigan. "The truth is, there would be no center without the Foundation—they've consistently supported FiftyForward with substantial annual grants each year and capital gifts when needed, and it's made all the difference for this community."

Among the most popular daily activities are exercise classes, including yoga, aerobics, weight training and dancing. Also included are special interest clubs dedicated to activities such as gardening, billiards, genealogy, and two talented musical groups: the Silver Notes Band and the Golden Tones Choir.

"Many of our participants would suffer greatly without the center, and it's a blessing in their lives," Jernigan says. "That's the impact that an organization like the Memorial Foundation can have. It's become the model for philanthropy in Nashville and beyond."

"Abe's Garden is the first memory care community in the U.S. dedicated to providing and elevating the quality of the full spectrum of memory care for those with Alzheimer's."

—MICHAEL SHMERLING

FOUNDER

ABE'S GARDEN

The seeds of Abe's Garden were planted when founder Michael Shmerling's father, Abram "Abe" Shmerling, M.D., was diagnosed with Alzheimer's disease. Dealing with the disease firsthand, Michael witnessed the limited availability of quality services and care dedicated to a rapidly growing population of elderly adults.

Michael's passion for establishing an Alzheimer's Center of Excellence in Nashville grew daily as the family watched, virtually helpless, as their father suffered for more than eleven years, finally succumbing to the disease in November of 2006.

"Throughout my father's battle with Alzheimer's, the idea for Abe's Garden began to take root," Shmerling says. "There were no proven treatments or cures, so the only thing we could do was find a way to improve the quality of life for patients and their families."

Projections of longer life expectancies and the lack of care available demonstrated an imminent need. Not only did Middle Tennessee need a respite care and residential living option for individuals, but also a center of knowledge. Abe's Garden set out with a mission to improve the lives of patients, affected families, and professional care partners.

The LEED-certified campus, which includes a three-acre park and interactive gardens, allows residents to age in a familiar environment throughout all stages of cognitive health—from day care, to respite, to residential, to end of life. Individualized programming incorporates pets, exercise, art and music, among others, reflective of activities that residents participated in during earlier phases of their lives.

"I remember Mr. Elliott stating very succinctly that this facility would provide hope. Not only did the Foundation support the Memory Care Center for Excellence with funding, but they also legitimized our campaign to other funders. Abe's Garden would not have been possible were it not for the Memorial Foundation," says Shmerling.

"Alive Hospice provides loving care to people with life-threatening or terminal illnesses, support to their families, and service to the community in a spirit of enriching lives."

—ANNA-GENE O'NEAL

PRESIDENT & CEO

ALIVE HOSPICE

Founded in Middle Tennessee in November 1975, Alive Hospice was only one year behind the first hospice program to be started in the United States. Through grassroots movements, other hospices began appearing across the country, unified by compassionate people committed to helping patients live in comfort until death occurred, and to helping families grieve with support.

The non-profit was chartered with three core goals: providing comprehensive care to terminally ill patients and their families; offering support for grieving adults and children; and serving the community as a center for research and education. Today, that means that more than 3,600 patients and their families annually in Middle Tennessee – four hundred fifty-plus each day – are under Alive's hospice care, while six hundred adults and children benefit from grief support services, and tomorrow's caregivers are trained and the community educated on terminal illness, end of life, and grief.

"To say it simply, the impact of the Memorial Foundation on our organization has been monumental, and through that support we've been able to invest in the community and have a greater impact in providing end of life care and grief support services for the entire community," says Alive Hospice President & CEO Anna-Gene O'Neal, RN, MSN, MBA. "When you look at the array of projects, from capital to counseling, that they have helped fund, you realize they understand it's not just about ensuring we have those services available today, but in the future."

Recognizing that a significant portion of those dealing with the loss of loved ones are children, the Memorial Foundation supported the pediatric grief services program, including a summer camp, and most recently the new Simulation Lab at Alive Hospice opened in 2016, allowing for more accurate teaching and training in end of life conversations.

"End of life conversations are not something that see much attention in traditional health sciences training, but end of life is a natural and incredibly meaningful aspect of life; understanding that concept is so important to healing," O'Neal says. "There is nothing like this available in the United States, and we're inviting members of the clinical community to participate and seeing great outcomes. It would not have been possible without the Memorial Foundation."

"

Discovery Place exists to guide men from the depths of addiction to the joy of recovery.

—JOE MORGAN

FOUNDER

"

DISCOVERY PLACE

Honesty. Perseverance. Discipline. Tolerance. Love. Those principles are the foundation of a sober, happy, useful, and whole life. Discovery Place was founded in 1997 as a 24-bed residential recovery program, priced affordably and willing to work with anyone seeking to overcome addiction. The thirty-day program that started in Burns, Tennessee, has since added a twelve-bed campus in Dickson, and over the last two decades has helped more than 3,200 men find sobriety.

"I am a recovering alcoholic, and I realized that the disease is mental, physical and spiritual," says Discovery Place Founder Joe Morgan. "This is a spiritual retreat based on the twelve-step program of Alcoholics Anonymous, and we wanted to offer that at a cost so the money wouldn't be a barrier to recovery. We wouldn't be here without the help of the Memorial Foundation, and particularly the influence of Drew Maddux."

An experienced staff introduces each guest and his family to the principles of the twelve-step recovery program in a beautiful countryside setting. Upon completion, they will have gained a clear understanding of the disease of alcohol and drug addiction, and have discovered how to recover by applying the principles one day at a time.

"We've had about 6,500 men go through the program since 1997, and there were certainly times when we were very close to not being able to make it. The Memorial Foundation was instrumental in helping us succeed, and now our success rates are over sixty percent. It's been a blessing to a lot of families."

"Faith Family's mission is to provide the residents of greater Nashville who are uninsured or underinsured with affordable, quality primary medical care."

—LAURA HOBSON

PRESIDENT & CEO

FAITH FAMILY MEDICAL CENTER

Faith Family Medical Center's approach to providing medical services for the uninsured and underinsured is unique—more than 160 physicians have agreed to offer primary and specialized care for the program's patients, as long as participants work twenty hours a week or are attending school full-time.

"Our focus is on treating patients physically, mentally, and spiritually," says Faith Family Medical Center President & CEO Laura Hobson. "The recent changes in health insurance provided coverage to a lot of people, but they don't always have the funds to cover the high deductibles. We charge on a sliding fee scale and are able to subsidize through donations."

From its clinic on 21st Avenue in Nashville, just between St. Thomas Midtown and Centennial hospitals, Faith Family sees 60 to 75 new patients a month, and has treated more than 35,000 Nashvillians through 15 years in operation. Services have expanded over time to include a wellness component that is now integral to the Journey to Health program, where a registered dietician oversees educational initiatives around nutrition, cooking, exercise, and a community garden.

Founding Medical Director Tom Henderson, M.D., says the Memorial Foundation's support was instrumental in establishing the clinic.

"Faith Family would not be where it is today without that generous support," Henderson says. "J.D. Elliott recognized the need very early on, and the Foundation's staff has continued to follow that path of vision and service that J.D. forged for so many worthwhile organizations throughout Middle Tennessee."

HOME BOUND MEALS

Five days a week, volunteers package and deliver 120 meals and deliver them to seniors and others who can't properly feed themselves. Working with the Mid-Cumberland Human Resource Agency, this "Meals on Wheels" program takes referrals from social workers, doctors and nurses, physical rehabilitation centers, and neighbors who recognize the need for nutrition that may not otherwise be met.

"It's not about economic status—we will serve any senior citizen in Hendersonville, and others under sixty who may need that support," says Home Bound Meals Board Chair Tommy Decker. "It may be someone who has been receiving chemotherapy or was just discharged from the hospital. We conduct an assessment of their health and situation, and there are a lot of people stuck at home who can't take care of themselves very well."

The meals—typically a meat with two vegetables, bread, a dessert and milk—are designed by a registered dietician, packaged into individual portions and delivered warm across seven different routes at lunchtime during the week. More than a hundred volunteers play a role in preparing and distributing the meals, which cost $4.71 each. Recipients are not required to contribute, but some do. The rest is covered by private funders like the Memorial Foundation.

"The hard work is done by our amazing volunteers, but we have to raise the money to sustain the program. The Memorial Foundation has believed in our mission and wanted us to continue serving more and more people, and their support has been so powerful," Decker says.

Interfaith Dental Clinic provides affordable dental services for uninsured, elderly, and low-income working people and families.

—RHONDA SWITZER-NADASDI, DMD

CEO

INTERFAITH DENTAL CLINIC

After volunteering as a dentist in third-world countries, Interfaith Dental Clinic Founder Dr. Tom Underwood realized that hardworking people in Middle Tennessee were in as desperate need of care. They just couldn't afford it.

With the help of the Nashville Dental Society and the West End United Methodist Church, Interfaith Dental Clinic opened in 1994 with two chairs and one employee in the basement of the church, offering affordable care on a sliding fee scale for working poor families and the elderly who were falling between the cracks of private practice and public health care.

Twenty years later, the clinic has grown to two locations and eighteen chairs, serving more than 2,500 people a year from its state-of-the-art facilities on Patterson Street in Nashville and in Rutherford County. Working primarily with employed patients who are experiencing poverty, Interfaith's nighttime hours and highly trained volunteers provide opportunities that not only help people get healthy, but step out of the shadows.

Interfaith CEO Rhonda Switzer-Nadasdi, DMD, says that not only has the Memorial Foundation been there as a funder since the beginning, but they've done it in a unique and impactful way.

"Our growth and impact can be traced back to the beginning of that relationship, and that support has added such credibility to our work and helped us leverage other funders to get involved," Switzer-Nadasdi says. "It's more than oral health. It's overall health, and economic heath that opens doors that wouldn't open before. Your smile says something about your class that you can't hide, can't put clothes on or even improve with an education. It's a significant part of new starts and recovery, and reaching God-given potential."

Men of Valor is committed to winning men in prison to Jesus Christ and and equipping them to re-enter society as men of integrity — becoming givers to the community rather than takers.

—OVERTON THOMPSON III

BOARD CHAIRMAN

MEN OF VALOR

National statistics show that 70 percent of men released from prison will return. But through Bible-based programming, aftercare and re-entry services, and the work of dedicated staff and volunteers, Nashville's Men of Valor program has shattered those numbers. In fact, for men who complete the non-profit organization's six-month program inside the prison and twelve-month program after release, the recidivism rate is less than 15 percent.

Founder Carl Carlson was raised in orphanages and foster homes, and started doing "time" when he was just ten years old. The honorably discharged Vietnam veteran turned his own fifteen-year prison sentence into something positive when he founded Men of Valor in 1997, and the one-man show now has a staff of eighteen and more than a hundred volunteers changing the lives of about 250 men each year.

Carl's dream before he passed in 2014 was to create a residential campus where men re-entering society could find the hope and stability needed to overcome the odds.

"The Memorial Foundation has been a key supporter of ours, including our facility currently under construction in Antioch," says Men of Valor Board Chair Overton Thompson III. "That campus will allow us to work intensively with the guys when they get out, because those first two years are the most critical to ensuring they don't fall back into the same trap."

With established programs serving several prisons and the residential aftercare component on the horizon, Thompson says they cover the waterfront with services: a strong spiritual basis, substance abuse counseling and prevention, job readiness, parental and financial planning, and more.

"Our focus is on getting these guys' lives turned around and keeping them out of prison. Part of that is the continued training of our board and staff to maximize our effectiveness, and the Memorial Foundation has supported not only operations and capital projects but also underwrote a program through the Center for Non-profit Management to train executive directors and board chairs to be better governors of organizations like ours," Thompson says. "Their impact on our organization and the city has been phenomenal, almost incalculable.

"It just shows how much they care about making a difference, and we certainly couldn't have accomplished what we have without them."

" The Nashville Food Project aims to bring people together to grow, cook, and share food for the homeless of Nashville, and create a community through this helping process.

—TERI SLOAN

DEVELOPMENT DIRECTOR

THE NASHVILLE FOOD PROJECT

A group of Nashvillians visiting Austin, Texas, in 2006 came across a mobile food ministry reaching homeless populations, and thus the Mobile Loaves & Fishes program was born in Nashville soon after. Three days a week, working from a church commissary, the food truck would run sack lunches to homeless camps.

That model has since evolved to The Nashville Food Project, which not only serves 3,000 made-from-scratch hot meals and snacks each week across the city, but has created a sustainable agriculture model with far-reaching benefits.

"The Memorial Foundation allowed us to become an independent organization, which really changed our model and set the stage for a more comprehensive view of the food system in our city," says The Nashville Food Project Development Director Teri Sloan. "In addition to being a cornerstone funder, they provide a lot of advice and perspective. They have seen what works and what doesn't in the non-profit community, and being able to have those conversations is so valuable."

In recent years, The Nashville Food Project has grown to support five gardens throughout the community, growing food for their programs while assisting low-income and refugee populations with nutrition and even entrepreneurial support. Nine farmers from Bhutan now grow at a Food Project garden and sell their produce at the Nashville Farmers Market. They count a restaurant and The Nashville Food Project's meals program as clients, and proceeds go directly to the refugee farmers.

"We utilize other non-profits to deliver meals, such as with after-school programs, gang prevention mentoring, job training, parenting, financial literacy and English-learner classes— we're able to provide a hot meal for the attendees, and it drives attendance and produces better outcomes for the classes," Sloan says. "It magnifies the impact. There's something special about sharing a meal that breaks down a lot of barriers."

The Nashville Rescue Mission is dedicated to helping the hungry, homeless, and hurting, restoring hope and transforming lives. Three times a day, 365 days a year, hot meals are prepared for the hungry, homeless, and hurting in our community. The Nashville Rescue Mission serves about 2,000 people each day, nourishing the body and spirit and providing hope for today, tomorrow, and eternity.

—REV. GLENN CRANFIELD

PRESIDENT AND CEO

NASHVILLE RESCUE MISSION

B eyond that most basic need of sustenance, the Nashville Rescue Mission helps individuals develop a personalized strategy to escape their current situation, with the understanding that God has a plan and a purpose for every person.

The Hope for Tomorrow program is an intense, comprehensive, Christ-centered counseling and care model designed to help men and women understand the reasons behind their struggle with addiction, homelessness, and other broken lifestyles—and what steps they need to take to rebuild their lives on a solid foundation rooted in God's Word and long-lasting solutions.

The Mission's program doesn't focus on just one part of a person's life—they believe it's important to affect a person's entire life—physical, mental, spiritual, emotional, and social. We are committed to restoring the whole person through a Christian approach that helps the homeless and addicted learn how much God loves them and gain the biblical insight they need to lead a productive life in and for Christ.

"The Mission has received generous grants from the Memorial Foundation over the years to support our ministry to the hungry, homeless and hurting in our community," says Rev. Glenn Cranfield, President and CEO of the Nashville Rescue Mission. "J.D. Elliott was a dear friend who is truly missed, and under the leadership of Scott Perry, they continue to support the work of so many local nonprofits.

"It's important that we all join together in finding solutions to the needs in our community that will improve the quality of life for everyone."

> "Oasis helps underserved youth navigate the tricky waters of teenage years with a wide array of programs designed to help them grow thrive and make positive change.."
>
> —TOM WARD
>
> PRESIDENT & CEO

OASIS CENTER

Founded in 1969 to provide community-based care for youth experiencing alcohol and drug problems, the Oasis Center has evolved over the past four decades into one of the nation's leading youth-serving organizations, offering safety and support to Nashville's most vulnerable and disconnected youth while seeking to also teach young people how to transform the conditions that create problems for them in the first place.

"We embrace our responsibility to change the odds in our community that will allow more young people to thrive and move into a healthy adulthood," says Oasis Center Executive Director Tom Ward. "These young people hold the keys to addressing some of the most challenging problems facing our city, but their lives are complex and and the approach has to be comprehensive."

Collectively, Oasis programs provide life-changing, intensive opportunities to nearly 3,000 youth and their families each year, while reaching thousands more through educational projects and presentations. In 2009, the Youth Opportunity Center opened its doors as a 39,000 square-foot facility unlike anything else in the Southeast, bringing nine youth agencies under the same roof to deliver crisis and residential services and more.

"These disenfranchised teens are scared when they are on the streets, so we're building a level of trust that allows us to support them in meaningful ways," Ward says. "The Memorial Foundation gets that, and they've always allowed for the flexibility that allows us to be creative and nimble in serving our mission. Through our entire journey they have partnered with us in so many ways, and they genuinely care about addressing the needs that aren't otherwise being met. The Memorial Foundation raises the tide for everyone, and the impact is huge."

> "PENCIL links community resources with Nashville Public Schools to help young people achieve academic success and prepare for life."

—ANGIE ADAMS

PRESIDENT & CEO

PENCIL

PENCIL was started in 1982 by community leaders who wanted to connect the business community with Metro Nashville Public Schools, recruiting professionals to support the city's public education system with resources and volunteers to tutor, mentor, and support students to increase their academic success.

"The Memorial Foundation was one of our earliest sponsors of the Reading Partners Program in 2000, connecting volunteers who work with students one-on-one for thirty minutes each week during the school year," says PENCIL Foundation President & CEO Angie Adams. "They play word games, work on vocabulary and pronunciation, and bring language and books to life."

More than anything, she says, it's about putting context to those words. Students may be able to read the text and pronounce it, but they don't know what it means. Since 2000, nearly 30,000 children have been touched by the program, which now serves twenty-five elementary schools and a handful of middle schools with more than a thousand volunteers each year.

"The benefits are clear, but the only way our model is economically viable is to partner with companies and organizations to help us recruit and manage this fleet of long-term volunteer reading partners, and make a large impact," Adams says. "The Memorial Foundation has not only been a steadfast supporter, but they've pushed us to move the dial even more. They want our city to be better, to understand what their investment is yielding and how else they can help, and that has raised the bar for the entire non-profit community."

"Siloam Family Health Center is dedicated to sharing the love of Christ by serving those in need through health care.

—MORGAN WILLS, MD

PRESIDENT & CEO

SILOAM FAMILY HEALTH CENTER

Siloam emerged from humble beginnings, but with a big vision. In 1989, a group of members of Nashville's Belmont Church were captivated by a holistic vision of the Kingdom of God that would make a real difference in real-world problems. It was a calling to provide a solution for people with limited resources, who were falling through the cracks of the conventional health care system. In 1991, Siloam Family Health Center was born as a volunteer-driven primary care clinic in the Edgehill neighborhood, serving the uninsured through the generosity of the community and allowing patients to contribute toward the cost of their care according to their capacity.

Today a staff of forty-three professionals and 400-plus volunteers treat about 5,000 patients a year from all over Middle Tennessee, addressing the physical, emotional, spiritual and social determinants of health in a well-equipped, 12,000 square-foot facility.

"There is no doubt that the Memorial Foundation has had a catalytic impact on our organization over the years, starting with a significant inaugural gift that allowed Siloam to hire its first executive director, Nancy West," says Siloam Family Health Center President & CEO Morgan Wills, MD. " Nancy and our board were able to leverage that inaugural gift, grow our tiny budget, and expand our impact exponentially. By the time I came on staff as a physician in 2000, we were seeing about 90 nationalities in our practice."

Wills says the ongoing support of the Foundation gave the staff the confidence and resources to realize they could make a meaningful difference for refugees and others without health insurance.

"The Memorial Foundation is like yeast in the dough of this city—if you took it out of the loaf, it would taste a lot flatter and rise a lot less! Aside from the critical financial support and the credibility that brings, I am particularly appreciative of the valuable counsel that J.D. Elliott and Scott Perry provided as I was transitioning from staff physician to the CEO role," Wills says. "They have had a transformative effect on thousands of people, and Nashville would be a much worse place without them."

"
The YMCA is a Christian-based mission aimed to strengthen foundations of communities and nurture those in it, as well as a chance for the children in these communities to learn and grow.
"

—KATHY RAGLIN

EXECUTIVE DIRECTOR

SUMNER COUNTY YMCA

When a capital campaign was launched in 1998 by a group of community leaders focused on building a YMCA to serve Sumner County, the most important objective was to find a suitable location. Among the first calls was one to the Memorial Foundation.

"That gift of a beautiful piece of property where our facility would be built marked the beginning of a twenty-year relationship with the Memorial Foundation that has allowed us to serve this entire area from 'cradle to grave,'" says Sumner County YMCA Executive Director Kathy Raglin. "As a result of that incredible gift, we were able to dedicate more resources to the facility, and it means so much to everyone who visits the Y every day."

Located just behind the Memorial Foundation's offices in Hendersonville, the Sumner County YMCA opened in 2000, and has since been utilized by hundreds of thousands of members. Children as young as six weeks and adults into their nineties use the facility, whether it be exercising, enjoying the pool, taking a fitness or enrichment class, watching the kids play sports, or simply playing cards with friends.

Raglin says for some seniors, it's not only an opportunity to stay active but to keep their minds sharp through interaction. Some of them were among those who helped make the facility possible years ago, and they now enjoy the benefits at another stage of life.

In 2004, the Memorial Foundation made another significant contribution to build a pavilion, including restroom and changing facilities, to be used for camps that serve about 170 kids a day each summer.

"We just celebrated our sixteenth year of operation, and it's an incredible thing to see this place have such a huge impact on so many people of all ages and interests," Raglin says. "It's just one of the many examples of how much the Memorial Foundation has contributed to this community."

> "For more than 30 years, the Tennessee Foreign Language Institute has been dedicated to meeting the intercultural communication needs of government, industry, commerce, education and individuals through language classes, training, translation and interpretation services.
>
> — JANICE RODRIGUEZ
> EXECUTIVE DIRECTOR

TENNESSEE FOREIGN LANGUAGE INSTITUTE

Recognizing the critical need for government employees to build foreign language skills, understand the most effective teaching methodologies, and spread that knowledge throughout all levels of Tennessee's public education system, the state legislature established the Tennessee Foreign Language Institute in 1986. Today, the Institute receives about 20 percent of its funding from the state, while revenue from clients and private supporters like the Memorial Foundation provide the rest.

A staff of about twenty-five educators and administrators from six different countries offer foreign language classes, high-quality instruction to English language learners, and interpretation and translation services to thousands of state employees and citizens each year.

Among the first partnerships with the Memorial Foundation was ESL to Go, a classroom on wheels that overcame the transportation barrier for immigrants and refugees and provides free English classes that help ease their transition into a new culture.

"The Memorial Foundation recognized the vision and what it could do for Nashville, helped us evaluate what it would take to be successful, then provided funding for the mobile classroom and operations dollars to help support the program," says TFLI Executive Director Janice Rodriguez. "It was less about a formula and more about understanding the need, which is unique in our experience with funders, and the result has been a tremendous success."

Next came Camp Illuminate, a summer English learning opportunity for middle schoolers that combines learning and technology for non-native residents in an environment that cultivates self-discovery and a greater understanding of the city they now call home.

"The input and feedback on our programs have been so beneficial, and it's clear that the staff and board of the Memorial Foundation have a genuine concern for seeing us succeed and leveraging their dollars for the benefit of the community," Rodriguez says. "Working with them is so fulfilling—they take the time to know what the impact will be, and in turn, we get to build relationships with people who care deeply about this city and truly making a difference."

> The Next Door Inc. provides a continuum of evidence-based services for women and their families impacted by addiction, mental illness, trauma and/or incarceration with Christ-centered compassionate care.
>
> —LINDA LEATHERS
>
> CEO

THE NEXT DOOR

In the spring of 2002, a small group of women from First Baptist Church in Nashville—who called themselves the "Wild Group of Praying Women"—felt compelled to use a vacant building in downtown Nashville to somehow support the less fortunate. After conducting a survey of local leaders, they realized there was a gap in the system when it came to helping women who were released from local jails or prisons.

"We met with a local warden who explained that after a woman paid her dues to society, she far too often went back to addiction and then returned to incarceration within months, even weeks," says Linda Leathers, CEO of The Next Door. "It's a heartbreaking cycle. We decided to provide these women a 'next door' to experience a fresh start and offer hope."

The founders designed a residential transitional program to address the physical, mental and spiritual needs of women coming from incarceration, and The Next Door was born. The team soon realized addiction was a monumental problem within the population they served. To accommodate the need, they added treatment services to their ministry. Currently, at its campus off of Charlotte Avenue, a professional team of counselors, case managers, nurse practitioners, masters-level social workers, interns, mentors and job coaches provide comprehensive care for women and their families from all walks of life.

They offer an array of services, including medically monitored detox, inpatient and outpatient services, family counseling programs and a permanent residential complex where clients and their families can live as they continue their recovery. This year, the organization will serve over 1,000 women and families.

Leathers says the Memorial Foundation was the first to invest in their vision over a decade ago.

"We had a plan and a building, but we had a lot to learn. They believed in us and helped build capacity along the way as a very strategic partner to The Next Door," she says. "It's truly a partnership. They make us feel like we're the only non-profit in the world when we get together.

"We always leave our meetings having gained new wisdom and with a smile of encouragement on our faces. They don't always say "yes," but we know they believe in us and that they will help us succeed. That's a great feeling."

"Adventure Science Center is an independent, not-for-profit educational institution dedicated to igniting curiosity and inspiring the lifelong discovery of science since 1945."

—TINA BROWN

INTERIM CEO

ADVENTURE SCIENCE CENTER

The Children's Museum of Nashville was first established in 1944, on 2nd Avenue South in downtown Nashville. World War II was coming to and end and the nation was beginning to look to the future. Sergeant John Ripley Forbes' vision for Nashville's future was focused on children, and his enthusiasm for a children's museum sparked the involvement of some of the city's most influential citizens, the building was leased and the museum opened its doors on Halloween 1945.

Seven years later, first planetarium in Tennessee was opened, and in 1974, the museum moved to the location on Fort Negley Boulevard. The organization's name changed over the years, most recently from Cumberland Science Museum to Adventure Science Center in November 2002. Now with 44,000 square feet of exhibit space, the Center features nearly 175 hands-on exhibits focused on biology, physics, visual perception, listening, mind, air and space, energy and earth science.

About 300,000 visitors each hear enjoy science demonstrations, and the Sudekum Planetarium's state-of-the-art digital projection and surround sound help enhance multi-media programs covering a wide range of sciences, history, culture and laser shows. Adventure Science Center Interim CEO Tina Brown says the Memorial Foundation has been there every step of the way.

"Over the years, the Memorial Foundation's support—both monetary and managerial—has been integral to our ability to inspire the lifelong discovery of science," Brown says. "In addition to significant program support, they have funded major exhibit expansions such as the Space Chase Gallery, which teaches us why we go to space and what we learn there, and most recently, our Innovation Incubator, a maker space with intrigues people who like to create, invent and learn.

Most importantly, Mr. Eliott led the effort to bring together the healthcare community in 2005 to provide the inspiration and funding for our BodyQuest gallery. That support has been a spark on so many meaningful levels."

> "Safe Haven Family Shelter empowers Middle Tennessee homeless families with children to achieve lasting self sufficiency."
>
> —JOYCE LAVERY
>
> PRESIDENT AND CEO

SAFE HAVEN FAMILY SHELTER

In 2003, two non-profits serving the homeless merged into one, driven by the belief that parents and children must be kept together in order to ensure security, success and self-sufficiency. The Memorial Foundation has supported Safe Haven Family Shelter from the beginning, but President and CEO Joyce Lavery remembers the year 2009 as a pivotal moment.

"That gift came at a time when we needed it most. They understood the need and that we were the only ones addressing it," Lavery says. "The Memorial Foundation believed in us and the work we were doing, and that gift allowed us to do some strategic planning and really turned the tide for our organization."

Safe Haven set a goal to work with as many as one hundred families a year, with ten in the residential program and others transitioning to permanent housing. They have met that goal each of the last three years, Lavery says, and are seeing generational shifts as a result.

"This is not just a shelter, but a landing place of stability when they have no place else to go, and the family can stay together," she says. "We work with the children in a way that allows the parents to be more successful, and we provide compassionate care, develop an employment plan and secure affordable housing.

"The Memorial Foundation held us accountable, pushed us to constantly improve, and as a result we have been able to help a lot of people get off the streets and back on their feet."

"The Salvus Center is a faith-based health center that provides dental and medical care for those who are working an uninsured.

—SHELLEY AMES

EXECUTIVE DIRECTOR

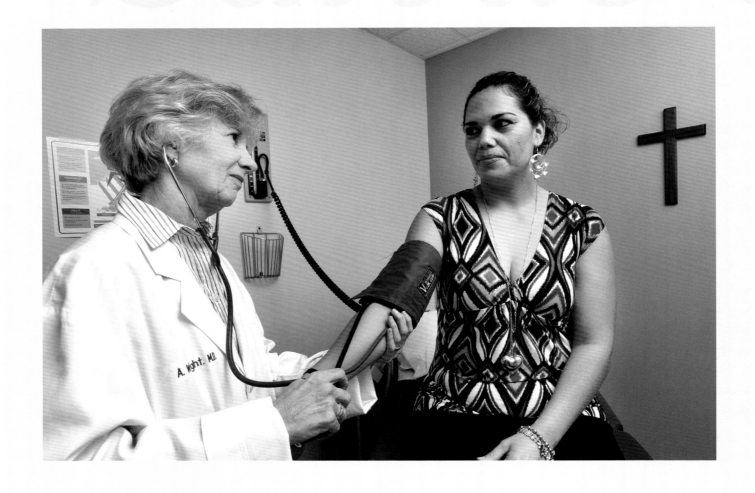

SALVUS CENTER

When a group of Sumner County residents came together in 2004 with an idea to establish a medical clinic to serve those without health insurance, the Memorial Foundation was the first donor to support the vision. The Salvus Center opening the following year, providing medical and dental care as a "hand-up" to people who were working but could not pay the high cost of healthcare.

Over the course of ten years, more than 43,000 patients have been seen in the clinic, which works closely with local hospitals, physicians, dentists and pharmacies to make it all possible. Nearly every specialty physician in Sumer County is involved in the delivery of care, along with more than twenty volunteer dentists.

"Our founders realized the need, and that a sinus infection doesn't belong in the ER," says Executive Director Shelley Ames. "Here, we develop a relationship with those patients and they trust us and know what to expect. They pay based on their ability, and they are able to experience wholeness, wellness and healing with Salvus Center as their primary care facility. Seeing the whole healthcare system of our community come together to make this possible was an incredible thing, and the Memorial Foundation made it possible."

Ames says it's about helping people be well so they can go to work and keep a roof over their heads and food on their tables.

"We are so proud of what we've been able to accomplish together," Ames says. "And that includes our patients. Everyone is working together, giving some and pulling their weight, and that creates a win-win situation."

“ Second Harvest Food Bank works to feed hungry people and solve hunger issues
in Middle and West Tennessee. ”

—JAYNEE DAY

PRESIDENT & CEO

SECOND HARVEST FOOD BANK

When America's first food bank was established in Phoenix in the mid-'70s, a model emerged for local organizations to collect and distribute food that would otherwise be wasted. With the support of several community leaders, Nashville's Second Harvest Food Bank opened in 1978, inspecting and sorting 160,000 pounds of food that first year and distributing it to soup kitchens, pantries and shelters serving the hungry.

Over the last forty years, the original purpose has not changed: to be a central hub for companies, groups and individuals who wish to help provide food for hungry people in Middle Tennessee. But today, Second Harvest has grown to be one of the largest and most comprehensive of 200 food banks and distribution centers nationwide.

Last year, Second Harvest distributed more than thirty million pounds of food 490 partner agencies, providing twenty-six million meals to hungry children, families and seniors throughout service area that covers forty-six counties in Middle and West Tennessee.

"The Memorial Foundation has been instrumental since its inception in helping Second Harvest Food Bank of Middle Tennessee be successful in carrying out its mission to feed hungry people and work to solve hunger issues in our community," says Second Harvest President & CEO Jaynee Day. "Not only has the Foundation continued to provide yearly operating support, but it was also one of the first funders to support our capital campaign effort to expands and improve our delivery of services to those in need. That support has provided hope to those who struggle daily with issues of hunger, and for that we are truly thankful and grateful."

> " The American Red Cross prevents and alleviates human suffering in the face of emergencies
> by mobilizing the power of volunteers and the generosity of donors. "
>
> —JOEL SULLIVAN
> EXECUTIVE DIRECTOR

NASHVILLE AREA RED CROSS

From Friday, April 30 through Sunday, May 2, 2010, Nashville saw records for rainfall shattered, and the city was inundated with flooding in areas not in what was traditionally considered the floodplain. And while fortunately no lives were lost, the damage to property was staggering: thousands of Nashvillians were affected, losing cars, homes, schools, businesses and places of worship. But the citizens stood firm, with the help of the non-profit community.

Joel Sullivan, executive director of the Nashville Area Red Cross, remembers the event well.

"J.D. Elliott called me during the event with $50,000 from the Memorial Foundation, which was critical to our immediate disaster relief efforts," Sullivan says. "We were opening shelters while the floodwaters were still rising, and that means cots, blankets, pillows, food, baby formula and diapers, dry clothing, you name it. In total, we provided about $6 million in flood relief, but the timing of that donation was so important."

When disaster strikes, the Red Cross is prepared with humanitarian effort, which goes beyond shelters to helping people clean up their property, get healthy and get back on their feet. They assess the damage and who is affected, coordinate volunteers and logistics, collect and distribute relief materials and more.

"The Memorial Foundation has always been so good at assessing need, which has made us great partners," Sullivan says. "They focus on results, ask questions, challenge us, because they care. This city is much better off thanks to the work of the foundation."

1996–2016
GRANTEE LISTING

A Soldier's Child

A.B.L.E. Youth

A.C.T.I.O.N. Program

Abe's Garden

About Face Assemblies

ACE Nashville

Achilles International - Nashville Chapter

Adventist Community Services Center

Adventure Science Center

Affordable Housing Resources

African Leadership

Against the Grain

AGAPE

Agricultural Museum Association

Akiva School

Alcohol and Drug Council of Middle Tennessee

ALIAS Chamber Ensemble

Alignment Nashville

Alive Hospice

All About Women

All God's Children

All Together Madison

Alpha Delta Omega Foundation

ALS Association Tennessee Chapter

Alzheimer's Association-Mid South Chapter

Amazing Grace Mission of Sumner County

Amazing Grace Recovery Program

American Association of Refugee and Immigrant Women

American Baptist College

American Cancer Society-Greater Nashville Area

American Diabetes Association-Middle Tennessee Office

American Heart Association-Greater Southeast Affiliate

American Lung Association of Tennessee

American Parkinson Disease Association, Middle Tennessee Chapter

American Red Cross-Nashville Area Chapter

Andrew Jackson Foundation

Angel Heart Farm

Aphesis House

Aquinas College

Ark Community Resource & Assistance Center

Arthritis Foundation-Tennessee

Arts & Business Council of Greater Nashville

Arts At The Airport Foundation

Assistance League of Nashville

Association of Nonprofit Executives

Athletes in Action-Nashville

Autism Foundation of Tennessee

Autism Society of Middle Tennessee

Backfield in Motion

Baptist Homes for Exceptional Persons

Baptist Hospital Foundation

Barefoot Republic

Be A Helping Hand Foundation

Be Ye Kind One To Another

Becoming Like Christ

Beech Elementary PTO

Beech Senior High School

Beech Senior High School Parent Network

Begin Anew

Belcourt Theatre

Belle Meade Plantation

Belmont Mansion Association

Belmont University

Benton Hall School

Best Buddies Tennessee

Bethany Christian Services of Middle Tennessee

Bethesda Community Development Corporation

Bethlehem Centers of Nashville

Better Health 4Kids

Better Tomorrows Adult Education Center

Big Brothers Big Sisters of Middle Tennessee

Blakemore Children's Center

Bledsoe's Lick Historical Association

Book 'em

Bootstraps Foundation

Bordeaux Beautiful

Bordeaux Community Development Corporation

Bordeaux Hospital Advocates

Box 55 Association

Boys & Girls Clubs of Middle Tennessee

Brain Injury Association

Brain Tumor Foundation for Children

Bransford Youth & Community Development Center

Bridge Nashville

Bridges Academy

Bridges Domestic Violence Center

Bright Horizons Foundation for Children

Buffalo Valley

Building Lives Foundation

Byrum-Porter Senior Center

C.O.P.E. (Cooperative Outreach for Personal Emergencies)

Cable Foundation

Caldwell Early Childhood Center

Camp Marymount

Camp Sycamore Creek

Carpenter's Square

CASA

CASA of Robertson County

Catholic Charities of Tennessee

Center for Health Services

Center for Living and Learning

Center for Nonprofit Management

Center for Refugees and Immigrants of Tennessee

Center for Women in Medicine

Centerstone Military Services

Centerstone of Tennessee

Chadwell Elementary School

Character Counts! Nashville

Charis Health Center

Charles Davis Foundation

Cheatham County Long Term Recovery Organization

Cheatham Literacy Council

Cheekwood

Child Advocacy Center Wilson County and the 15th Judicial District

Child Care Alliance

ChildCare Tennessee

Children Are People

Children First Preschool

Christ Centered Ministries

Christian Community Outreach Center

Christian Community Schools

Christian Community Services

Christian Cooperative Ministry

Christian Leadership Concepts

Christian Towers of Gallatin

City of Gallatin

City of Goodlettsville

City of Hendersonville

City of Life

City of Millersville

City of Ridgetop Fire Department

Clean Air Partnership of Middle Tennessee

Coalition for Quality Children's Media

Cohn Adult High School

Communities In Schools of Tennessee

Community Care Fellowship

Community Career Center

Community Child Care Services

Community Concerts

Community Enhancement Centers

Community Food Advocates

Community Resource Center

Community Spirit

CommunityNashville

COMPASS

Compassionate Friends

Comprehensive Care Center

Concert Chorale of Nashville

Conexion Americas

Congressional Medal of Honor Foundation

Consumer Credit Counseling of Middle Tennessee, Inc.

Cottage Cove Urban Ministries

Council of Community Services

Council on Aging of Middle Tennessee

Country Day Montessori School

Country Music Hall of Fame and Museum

Create Nashville

Creating an Environment of Success

Creative Artists of Tennessee

Creative Youth Ministries

Creator's Kids Preschool

Crieve Hall Youth Athletic Association

Crimebusters, USA

Crittenton Services

CrossBRIDGE

Crossroads Campus

Cumberland Crisis Pregnancy Center

Cumberland Heights Foundation

Cumberland Pediatric Foundation

Cumberland Region Tomorrow

Cumberland River Compact

Cumberland Trail Conference

Cumberland University

Cumberland View Towers

Currey Ingram Academy

Dance Theatre of Tennessee

Davidson Academy

Davidson County Juvenile Court

Davidson County Sheriff's Office

Daystar Counseling Ministries

Decisions, Choices & Options

Developmental Learning Center

Disabled American Veterans-Chapter 3

Disciples Village of Nashville

Discover Madison

Discovery Place

Dismas

Dispensary of Hope

Domestic Violence Intervention Center (closed 09)

Donelson Christian Academy

Donelson Playground

Don't Follow Me

Down Syndrome Association of Middle Tennessee

Dress for Success Nashville

East Academy

East Nashville Center for the Creative Arts

East Nashville Cooperative Ministry

East Nashville High Alumni Association

East Nashville Hope Exchange

East Nashville R/UDAT

East Nashville Synergy Center

Easter Seals Tennessee

Eastland Christian Haven

Eating Disorders Coalition of Tennessee

Ed Temple Memorial Statue

Education First Fund

Eighteenth Avenue Family Enrichment Center

Employee Care Fund

Empower Me Day Camp

Encouragement Ministries

End Slavery Tennessee

Ennix-Jones Community Outreach Center

Epilepsy Foundation of Middle and West Tennessee

Equal Chance for Education

Evergreen Life Services

Executive Women International-Nashville Chapter

Explorastory of Sumner County

Faces of Hope Children's Therapy Center

Faith Family Medical Center

Family & Children's Service

Family Action Council of Tennessee

Family Affair Ministries

Family Foundation Fund

Family Reconciliation Center

Fannie Battle Day Home for Children

Feed America First of Tennessee

Fellowship of Christian Athletes

Fifteenth Avenue Baptist Church

Fifteenth Avenue Baptist Church Child Learning Center

Fifteenth Avenue Baptist Community Development Corporation

FiftyForward

FiftyForward Bordeaux

FiftyForward Madison Station

Finished Up

First Priority of Middle Tennessee

First Steps

Fisk University

Fisk University Community Alliance

Fort Campbell Historical Foundation

Forward Sumner Economic Council

Foundations Associates

4:13 Strong

Franklin Road Academy

Friends Helping Friends Drop-In Center

Friends In General

Friends of Beaman Park

Friends of Bledsoe Creek State Park

Friends of Cheatham County Public Libraries

Friends of Metro Parks Girls Program

Friends of Radnor Lake

Friends of Shelby Park and Bottoms

Friends of the Arts and Literature in Sumner

Friends of the Park

Friends of TIPS (Tennessee Infant Parent Services)

Friends of Warner Parks

Friendship Community Outreach Center

Friendship House

Frist Center for the Visual Arts

Full Count Ministries

Fund for Strategic Opportunities

Gabe's My Heart

Gallatin Arts Council

Gallatin C.A.R.E.S.

Gallatin Child Care Center

Gallatin Day Care Center

Gallatin Downtown Library Committee

Gallatin Lions Club

Gallatin Senior Citizens

Gallatin Shalom Zone

Gene Brown Elementary School

General Commission on United Methodist Men

Genesis Learning Centers

Gilda's Club Nashville

Girl Scouts of Middle Tennessee

GirlForce

Girls on the Run Nashville

GivingMatters.com

Glencliff High School

Global Center

Global Education Center

Good Neighbor Mission

Goodlettsville Community Foundation

Goodlettsville Elementary School

Goodlettsville Help Center

Goodpasture Christian School

Goodwill Industries of Middle Tennessee

Gordon Jewish Community Center

Gospel Music Association

Grace Adult Homes

Grace M. Eaton Childcare Center

Grace Place Ministry

Grantmakers In Health

Greater Faith Community Action Corporation

Greater Gallatin

Green Fork Academy

Greenbrier Historical Society

Greenbrier Youth Sports Association

Greenways for Nashville

Greenways of Sumner County

Guardianship & Trusts Corporation

Guild Elementary School

H.B. Williams Elementary School

Habilitation and Training Services

Habitat for Humanity of Greater Nashville

Habitat for Humanity of Sumner County

Hadley Park Tennis Club

Hands On Nashville

Hands With Heart Foundation For Deaf Children

Harpeth Hall School

Harvest Hands Community Development Corporation

Hattie Cotton Elementary

Haven Clinic

Healing Arts Project

Healing Hands International

Healing Wings

HEALS for Kids Health Fair

Health Careers Foundation

HEAR Nashville

Hearing Bridges

Helping Hands

Hendersonville Chamber Foundation

Hendersonville High School Foundation

Hendersonville Inline Hockey Association

Hendersonville Performing Arts Company

Hendersonville Rotary Foundation

Hendersonville Samaritan Association

Hendersonville Soccer League

Hendersonville Young Life

High Hopes Development Center

Historic Rock Castle

Holly Street Day Care

Home Bound Meals Program

HomeSafe of Sumner, Wilson & Robertson Counties

Homeward Bound

Homework Hotline

Hope Beyond Hope

Hope Clinic for Women

Hope Community Development Corporation

HOPE Family Health Services

Hope Food Bank

HOPE Learning Center

Hope Smiles

Hosanna Ministries

Hospital Hospitality House of Nashville

House of Mercy

Housing Fund

Howard Elementary School

Humanities Tennessee

Hume-Fogg Academic High School

Hungry Ear Productions

Hunters Lane Comprehensive High School

Hunters Lane High School Community Education

Imagination Library of Middle Tennessee

Imagine Goodlettsville

In Full Motion

Indian Lake Elementary School

INROADS

Insight Counseling Centers

Interfaith Dental Clinic

Inter-Museum Council of Nashville

Intrepid College Prep

Isaac Litton Alumni Association

Isaac Litton Middle School

Jack Anderson Elementary

Jack Anderson PTO

Jags' Little Cub House Childcare and Learning Center

Jason Foundation

Jefferson Street United Merchants Partnership

Jobs for Life

Joelton Community Club

Jonah's Journey

Joy Ministries

Junior Achievement of Middle Tennessee

Junior League of Nashville

Kelly Miller Smith Center Against Abusive Behavior

Kids For A Clean Environment (Kids F.A.C.E.)

Kid's Kingdom

Kids Voting of Middle Tennessee

King's Daughters Child Development Center

King's Daughters' School of Maury County

KIPP Academy Nashville

Knox Doss Middle School at Drakes Creek

L.A.S. Therapy Network and Development Group

Ladies of Charity of Nashville

Lakeshore Estates

LEAD Public Schools

Leadership Donelson-Hermitage

Leadership Goodlettsville

Leadership Music

Leadership Nashville

Leah Rose Residence for Senior Citizens

Learning Plus Foundation

Legal Aid Society of Middle Tennessee and the Cumberlands

Leukemia & Lymphoma Society-Tennessee Chapter

Life of Victory Christian Ministries

Lighthouse Christian School

Lily's Garden

Lipscomb University

Literacy Council of Sumner County

Living Sent Ministries

Love Helps

Love In A Big World

Love Tennis

Madison Babe Ruth Baseball

Madison Campus Elementary

Madison Christian Medical Clinic

Madison Creek Elementary School PTO

Madison Little League

Madison School

Madison Tigers Youth Sports

Madison YMCA

Madison-Rivergate Area Chamber of Commerce

Make-A-Wish Foundation of Middle Tennessee

March of Dimes, Tennessee Chapter, Nashville Division

Martha O'Bryan Center

Martin Methodist College

Mary Parrish Center

Masonry Institute of Tennessee

Matthew 25

Matthew Walker Comprehensive Health Center

Mayor's Office of Children and Youth

McKendree Village

McNeilly Center for Children

MDHA Housing Trust Corporation

Meharry Medical College

Meharry-Vanderbilt Alliance Foundation

Men of Valor

Mending Hearts

Mental Health America of Middle Tennessee

Mercy Community Healthcare

Mercy Ministries of America

Merrol Hyde Magnet School

Merrol Hyde Magnet School Parent Teacher Organization

Metropolitan Board of Parks & Recreation

Metropolitan Development and Housing Agency

Metropolitan Educational Access Corporation

Metropolitan Nashville Arts Commission

Metropolitan Nashville General Hospital

Metropolitan Nashville Public Schools

Metropolitan Nashville Teachers' Apartments

Metropolitan Nashville/ Davidson County Public Schools

Mid-Cumberland Human Resource Agency

Middle Tennessee Council-Boy Scouts of America

Middle Tennessee Poison Center

Middle Tennessee School of Anesthesia

Minerva Foundation

Miriam's Promise

Mockingbird Theatre

Monroe Carell Jr. Children's Hospital at Vanderbilt

Monroe Harding

Montgomery Bell Academy

Morning Star Sanctuary

Moss Rose Education Foundation

Mothers Against Drunk Driving Tennessee

Mt. Juliet-West Wilson Senior Citizen's Center

Murrell School

Muscular Dystrophy Association - Nashville

Music City Legend

Music City Mystique

Music City Youth in the Arts

Music for Seniors

Music Health Alliance

My Friend's House Family & Children Services

N.A.P.S. Child Care

NAACP-Nashville Branch

NAMI Tennessee

NASBA Center for the Public Trust

Nashville Adult Literacy Council

Nashville Agency Collaboration

Nashville Ballet

Nashville Bar Foundation

Nashville CARES

Nashville Chamber Orchestra

Nashville Chamber Public Benefit Foundation

Nashville Chess Center

Nashville Children's Alliance

Nashville Children's Theatre

Nashville Civic Design Center

Nashville Clean Water Project

Nashville Committee on Foreign Relations

Nashville Conflict Resolution Center

Nashville District Management Corporation

Nashville Drug Court Support Foundation

Nashville Film Festival

Nashville Food Project

Nashville Information Consortium

Nashville Inner City Ministry

Nashville Institute for the Arts

Nashville International Center for Empowerment

Nashville Jazz Workshop

Nashville Opera

Nashville Opportunities Industrialization Center

Nashville Promise Neighborhood

Nashville Public Education Foundation

Nashville Public Library Foundation

Nashville Public Radio

Nashville Public Television

Nashville Repertory Theatre

Nashville Rescue Mission

Nashville School of Law

Nashville Shakespeare Festival

Nashville State Community College Foundation

Nashville Strip Church

Nashville Symphony Association

Nashville Tree Foundation

Nashville Youth Alliance

Nashville Youth for Christ

Nashville Zoo

NashvilleREAD

Nashville's Agenda

National Center for Fathering

National Hemophilia Foundation-Cumberland Chapter

National Museum of African American Music

National Society of the Colonial Dames in the State of Tennessee

Nations Ministry Center

NationsUniversity

Native American Indian Association of Tennessee

Nature Conservancy - Tennessee Chapter

NeedLink Nashville

Neely's Bend Elementary School

Neighborhood Justice Center (closed 09)

Neighborhoods Resource Center

New Horizons Corporation

New Transitions

Next Step

NowPlayingNashville.com

Number One Volunteer Fire Department

Nurses for Newborns of Tennessee

Oasis Center

Old Center Elementary School

On The Right Track Track Club

One Hundred Black Men of Middle Tennessee

100 Club of Sumner County

Open Table Nashville

Operation Andrew Group

Operation Dad 2008

Operation FINALLY HOME

Operation Stand Down Tennessee

Organized Neighbors of Edgehill

Oscar L. Farris Agricultural Museum Association

Our Kids

Outlook Nashville

Papillion Center for FASD

Parents Reaching Out

Park Center

PARTNERS

Partners for a Healthy Nashville

Peace Unlimited in Recovery

PearlPoint Cancer Support

PENCIL Foundation

People's Branch Theatre

Percy Priest Elementary

Pet Community Center

Planned Parenthood of Middle Tennessee

Pope John Paul II High School

Portland Area Library Foundation

Portland C.A.R.E.S.

Portland High School

Portland Preservation Foundation

Presbyterian Day School

Preston Taylor Ministries

Prevent Blindness Tennessee

Prevent Child Abuse Tennessee

Prison Fellowship Ministries

Progress

Project C.U.R.E.

Project for Neighborhood Aftercare

Project Play of Gallatin

Project Reflect

Project Return

Project S.H.A.R.E.

Project Transformation Tennessee

Prospect

Purpose Preparatory Academy

Real Families Real MOMS of East Nashville

RealSports Leadership Academy

REBOOT Combat Recovery

ReConstruct

Recovery Community

Refuge Center for Counseling

Rejoice Ministries

Renewal House

Residential Services

Restoration Community Outreach

ReUse Center

Robert E. Ellis Middle School

Robertson County Education Initiative

Robertson County Historical Society

Robertson County Players

Robertson County Reads

Robertson County Senior Center

Rochelle Center

Rock House Way

Rock the Street, Wall Street

Rocketown of Middle Tennessee

Ronald McDonald House Charities of Nashville, Tennessee

Rooftop Foundation

Room In The Inn

Rotary Club of Nashville

S.A.V.E. (Survivors Against Violent Environments)

Saddle Up!

Safe Haven Family Shelter

Safety Net Consortium of Middle Tennessee

Saint John Vianney Catholic School

Saint Thomas Family Health Center

Saint Thomas Health Services Fund

Salama Urban Ministries

Salvation Army-Nashville Area Command

Salvus Center

Samaritan Ministries

Scarritt-Bennett Center

Second Harvest Food Bank of Middle Tennessee

SECURE

Senior Center for the Arts

Senior Citizens of Hendersonville

Sexual Assault Center

Sharing the Vision

Shepherd's Center of Madison

Shepherd's Center of West End

Show Hope

Sign Club Co.

Silent Word Media Resources

Siloam Family Health Center

Simon Youth Foundation

Skyline Auxiliary

Social Enterprise Alliance-Nashville Chapter

Social Enterprise Catalyst

Soles4Souls

Songs for Sound

Sophia's Heart

Soul Harvest Outreach Ministries

Southeast Community Capital Corporation

Southeastern Council of Foundations

Southeastern Young Adult Book Festival

Southern Sudanese Youth Connection

Southern Word

Special Education Advocacy Center

Special Needs Sports Foundation

Special Olympics Tennessee

Spina Bifida Association of Middle Tennessee

Sponsors Scholarship Program

Sports 4 All Foundation

Spring Back Recycling

Springfield-Robertson County Emergency Food Bank

Spruce Street Golden Manor

St. Cecilia Congregation

St. Joseph Catholic School

St. Luke's Community House

St. Mary Villa Child Development Center

St. Timothy Tots Preschool Program

St. Vincent de Paul School (closed 09)

STARS Nashville

Station Camp High School

Stokes Brown Library

Stratford High School

Street Theatre Company

Sugarbugs

Sumner Academy

Sumner Child Advocacy Center - Ashley's Place

Sumner County Archives

Sumner County Board of Education

Sumner County CASA

Sumner County Government

Sumner County Health Committee

Sumner County Health Department

Sumner County Just Say No Network

Sumner County Museum

Sumner County NAACP

Sumner County Symphony

Sumner Mediation Services

Sumner Special Housing

Sumner Teen Center

T.R.A.C.

T.W. Hunter Middle School

Teach For America-Greater Nashville

Technology Access Center

Teen Challenge International-Nashville

Teen Court of Sumner County

Tennessean's Newspaper In Education

Tennessee Action Coalition

Tennessee Art Center at Madison

Tennessee Art League

Tennessee Association for the Education of Young Children

Tennessee Association of Alcohol, Drugs & Other Addiction Services

Tennessee Association of Business Foundation

Tennessee Association of Craft Artists

Tennessee Bar Association-Young Lawyers Division

Tennessee Breast Cancer Coalition

Tennessee Center for Nursing

Tennessee Central Railway Museum

Tennessee Christian Medical Center Foundation

Tennessee Coalition to End Domestic and Sexual Violence

Tennessee Dance Theatre

Tennessee Drug Awareness Council

Tennessee Economic Council on Women

Tennessee Environmental Council

Tennessee Foreign Language Institute Fund

Tennessee Golf Foundation

Tennessee Health Care Campaign

Tennessee Historical Commission Foundation

Tennessee Historical Society

Tennessee History for Kids

Tennessee Holocaust Commission

Tennessee Independent Colleges and Universities Association

Tennessee Justice Center

Tennessee Justice for Our Neighbors

Tennessee Kidney Foundation

Tennessee Legal Community Foundation

Tennessee Lions Charities

Tennessee Medical Education Fund

Tennessee Medical Foundation

Tennessee Nurses Foundation

Tennessee Parks and Greenways Foundation

Tennessee Performing Arts Center

Tennessee Players

Tennessee Police Athletic League

Tennessee Primary Care Association

Tennessee Prison Outreach Ministry

Tennessee SCORE (State Collaboration on Reforming Education)

Tennessee Secondary School Athletic Association

Tennessee Senior Olympics

Tennessee Sled Hockey Association

Tennessee Stars Senior 55

Tennessee State Museum Foundation

Tennessee State University

Tennessee Supreme Court Historical Society

Tennessee Theatre Company

Tennessee Voices for Children

Tennessee Voices for Victims

Tennessee Wildlife Federation

Tennessee Women's Theater Project

Tennessee-Kentucky Threshermen's Association

The Beat of Life

The Big Payback Middle Tennessee

The Bridge Ministry

The Brown Center for Autism

The Center for American Military Music Opportunities

The Center for Courageous Kids

The Community Foundation of Middle Tennessee

The Conservancy for the Parthenon and Centennial Park

The Contributor

The Edison School

The Family Center

The Foundation for Athletics in Nashville Schools

The Land Trust for Tennessee

The Nashville Choir

The New Beginnings Center

The Next Door

The Society of St. Andrew

Thistle Farms

Time to Rise

TNKids Nutrition

Touchstone Ministry

Transit Alliance of Middle Tennessee

Trevecca Nazarene University

Trousdale Place Historic Site

Trust for the Future

Tucker's House

23rd District Judicial Advocates

23rd Psalm Ministry

U-Grow Adventures

Ujima House

Union Elementary STEM and Demonstration School

Union University-Hendersonville Campus

United Cerebral Palsy of Middle Tennessee

United Ministries of Robertson County

United Neighborhood Health Services

United Way of Metropolitan Nashville

United Way of Sumner County

University Community Health Services

University of Tennessee College of Social Work

University of Tennessee Institute of Agriculture

University School of Nashville

Urban Green Lab

Urban Housing Solutions

Urban League of Middle Tennessee

Valley View Camp

Vanderbilt Bill Wilkerson Center

Vanderbilt Kennedy Center for Research on Human Development

Vanderbilt University School of Law-Legal Aid Society

Vanderbilt University School of Nursing

Vanderbilt-Ingram Cancer Center

Vena Stuart Elementary School

Vietnam Veterans of Sumner County Foundation

Village Cultural Arts Center

VITAL Center of Nashville

Volunteer State College Foundation

VSA Tennessee

W.O. Smith/Nashville Community Music School

W.O.M.E.N. (Women On Maintaining Education and Nutrition)

Walden's Puddle

Walk/Bike Nashville

Watkins College of Art, Design & Film

Wayne Reed Christian Childcare Center

WCTE, Upper Cumberland Public Television

Welcome Home Ministries

Westmeade Elementary School

Westminster Home Connection

Westmoreland High School

White House High School Gifted Team

White House Inn Library

White House Middle School

Whitten Elementary

Who U With? Ministries

William Patton Jr. Foundation

Willow Oak Center for Arts & Learning at Robertson County

Wilson County Board of Education

Wilson County Youth Ranch

Woodbine Community Organization

Workers' Dignity Project

World Relief Nashville

World War II Memorial Trust

Worldwide Drug Free Youth

YMCA of Middle Tennessee

You Have The Power...Know How To Use It

Young Leaders Council

Youth Encouragement Services

Youth Incorporated

Youth Life Foundation of Tennessee

Youth Villages

Youth Yellow Pages

YWCA of Nashville and Middle Tennessee

FOUNDING BOARD MEMBERS

Charles B. Beck, M.D.

L. Dale Beck, M.D.

Frank M. Bumstead

Varina F. Buntin

Edward C. Dunn

Charles W. Fentress

Walter Clay Gaines Sr.

Alice I. Hooker

Russ Kersten

Drew R. Maddux Sr.

J.G. (Jim) Martin Jr.

Herbert T. McCall, M.D.

David E. McKee, M.D.

Judge George C. Paine II

William P. Puryear

James A. Rainey

Garland Rose

Jo Sanders

Herbert M. Shayne

Leah Rose Werthan

Julie B. Williams

OFFICERS

William P. Puryear, Chairman

James A. Rainey, Vice Chairman

J.D. Elliott, President

William R. Willis, Secretary

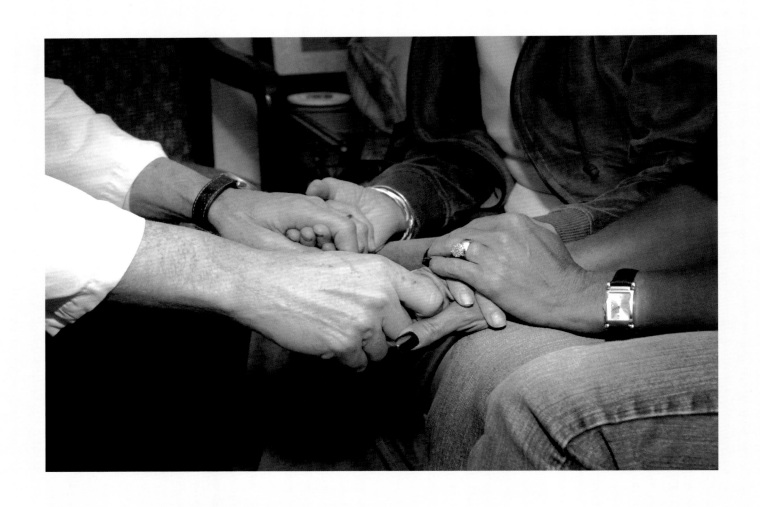

"IT IS NOT THE MAGNITUDE OF OUR ACTIONS

BUT THE AMOUNT OF LOVE THAT IS PUT INTO THEM THAT MATTERS."

—SAINT TERESA OF CALCUTTA